I0415748

January 2012

DESIGNING EVALUATIONS

2012 Revision

G A O
Accountability * Integrity * Reliability

Contents

Tables

Figures

Abbreviations

AEA	American Evaluation Association
GAGAS	generally accepted government auditing standards
GPRA	Government Performance and Results Act of 1993
NSF	National Science Foundation
OMB	Office of Management and Budget
SAMHSA	Substance Abuse and Mental Health Services Administration

Preface

GAO assists congressional decision makers in their deliberations by furnishing them with analytical information on issues and options. Many diverse methodologies are needed to develop sound and timely answers to the questions the Congress asks. To provide GAO evaluators with basic information about the more commonly used methodologies, GAO's policy guidance includes documents such as methodology transfer papers and technical guides.

This methodology transfer paper addresses the logic of program evaluation designs. It introduces key issues in planning evaluation studies of federal programs to best meet decision makers' needs while accounting for the constraints evaluators face. It describes different types of evaluations for answering varied questions about program performance, the process of designing evaluation studies, and key issues to consider toward ensuring overall study quality.

To improve federal program effectiveness, accountability and service delivery, the Congress enacted the Government Performance and Results Act of 1993 (GPRA), establishing a statutory framework for performance management and accountability, including the requirement that federal agencies set goals and report annually on progress towards those goals and program evaluation findings. In response to this and related management reforms, federal agencies have increased their attention to conducting program evaluations. The GPRA Modernization Act of 2010 raised the visibility of performance information by requiring quarterly reviews of progress towards agency and governmentwide priority goals. *Designing Evaluations* is a guide to successfully completing evaluation design tasks. It should help GAO evaluators—and others interested in assessing federal programs and policies—plan useful evaluations and become educated consumers of evaluations.

Designing Evaluations is one of a series of papers whose purpose is to provide guides to various aspects of audit and evaluation methodology and indicate where more detailed information is available. It is based on GAO studies and policy documents and program evaluation literature. To ensure the guide's competence and usefulness, drafts were reviewed by selected GAO, federal and state agency evaluators, and evaluation authors and practitioners from professional consulting firms. This paper updates a 1991 version issued by GAO's prior Program Evaluation and Methodology Division. It supersedes that earlier version and incorporates changes in federal program evaluation and performance measurement since GPRA was implemented.

We welcome your comments on this paper. Please address them to me at kingsburyn@gao.gov.

Nancy R. Kingsbury, Ph.D.
Managing Director
Applied Research and Methods

Chapter 1: The Importance of Evaluation Design

What Is a Program Evaluation?

A program evaluation is a systematic study using research methods to collect and analyze data to assess how well a program is working and why. Evaluations answer specific questions about program performance and may focus on assessing program operations or results. Evaluation results may be used to assess a program's effectiveness, identify how to improve performance, or guide resource allocation.

There is no standard government definition of "program." A program can be defined in various ways for budgeting and policy-making purposes. Whether a program is defined as an activity, project, function, or policy, it must have an identifiable purpose or set of objectives if an evaluator is to assess how well the purpose or objectives are met. Evaluations may also assess whether a program had unintended (perhaps undesirable) outcomes. An evaluation can assess an entire program or focus on an initiative within a program. Although evaluation of a federal program typically examines a broader range of activities than a single project, agencies may evaluate individual projects to seek to identify effective practices or interventions.

Program evaluation is closely related to performance measurement and reporting. Performance measurement is the systematic ongoing monitoring and reporting of program accomplishments, particularly progress toward preestablished goals or standards. Performance measures or indicators may address program staffing and resources (or inputs), the type or level of program activities conducted (or process), the direct products or services delivered by a program (or outputs), or the results of those products and services (or outcomes) (GAO 2011).

A program evaluation analyzes performance measures to assess the achievement of performance objectives but typically examines those achievements in the context of other aspects of program performance or in the context in which the program operates. Program evaluations may analyze relationships between program settings and services to learn how to improve program performance or to ascertain whether program activities have resulted in the desired benefits for program participants or the general public. Some evaluations attempt to isolate the causal impacts of programs from other influences on outcomes, whereas performance measurement typically does not. Evaluations have been used to supplement performance reporting by measuring results that are too difficult or expensive to assess annually or by exploring why performance goals were not met. (For examples, see GAO 2000.)

Why Conduct an Evaluation?

Federal program evaluation studies are typically requested or initiated to provide external accountability for the use of public resources (for example, to determine the "value added" by the expenditure of those resources) or to learn how to improve performance—or both. Evaluation can play a key role in strategic planning and in program management, providing feedback on both program design and execution.

Evaluations can be designed to answer a range of questions about programs to assist decision-making by program managers and policymakers. GAO evaluations are typically requested by congressional committees to support their oversight of executive branch activities. A committee might want to know whether agency managers are targeting program funds to areas of greatest need or whether the program as designed is, indeed, effective in resolving a problem or filling a need. The Congress might use this information to reallocate resources for a more effective use of funds or to revise the program's design.

The Congress also directly requests agencies to report on program activities and results. For example, legislative changes to a program might be accompanied by a mandate that the agency report by a specific date in the future on the effectiveness of those changes. Agencies may choose to design an evaluation to collect new data if they are unable to satisfy the request from available administrative data or performance reporting systems. They may also evaluate pilot or demonstration projects to inform the design of a new program.

GPRA performance reporting requirements were designed to provide both congressional and executive decision makers with more objective information on the relative effectiveness and efficiency of federal programs and spending. However, due to the influence of other factors, measures of program outcomes alone may provide limited information on a program's effectiveness. GPRA encourages federal agencies to conduct evaluations by requiring agencies to (1) include a schedule of future program evaluations in their strategic plans, (2) summarize their evaluations' findings when reporting annually on the achievement of their performance goals, and (3) explain why a goal was not met. Federal agencies have initiated evaluation studies to complement performance measures by (1) assessing outcomes that are not available on a routine or timely basis, (2) explaining the reasons for observed performance, or (3) isolating the program's impact or contribution to its outcome goals (GAO 2000).

Since 2002, the Office of Management and Budget (OMB) under the administrations of both Presidents Bush and Obama has set the expectation that agencies should conduct program evaluations. Initial OMB efforts to use agency performance reporting in decision making were frustrated by the limited quantity and quality of information on results (GAO 2005). Although federal program performance reporting improved, in 2009 OMB initiated a plan to strengthen federal program evaluation, noting that many important programs lacked evaluations and some evaluations had not informed decision making (OMB 2009).

Who Conducts Evaluations?

A federal program office or an agency research, policy or evaluation office may conduct studies internally, or they may be conducted externally by an independent consulting firm, research institute, or independent oversight agency such as GAO or an agency's Inspector General. The choice may be based on where expertise and resources are available or on how important the evaluator's independence from program management is to the credibility of the report. The choice may also depend on how important the evaluator's understanding of the program is to the agency's willingness to accept and act on the evaluation's findings.

For example, evaluations aimed at identifying program improvement may be conducted by a program office or an agency unit that specializes in program analysis and evaluation. Professional evaluators typically have advanced training in a variety of social science research methods. Depending on the nature of the program and the evaluation questions, the evaluation team might also require members with specialized subject area expertise, such as labor economics. If agency staff do not have specialized expertise or if the evaluation requires labor-intensive data collection, the agency might contract with an independent consultant or firm to obtain the required resources. (For more information, see U.S. Department of Health and Human Services 2010.)

In contrast, evaluations conducted to provide an independent assessment of a program's strengths and weaknesses should be conducted by a team independent of program management. Evaluations purchased by agencies from professional evaluation firms can often be considered independent. Conditions for establishing an evaluator's independence include having control over the scope, methods, and criteria of the review; full access to agency data; and control over the findings, conclusions, and recommendations.

Why Spend Time on Design?

Evaluators have two basic reasons for taking the time to systematically plan an evaluation: (1) to enhance its quality, credibility, and usefulness and (2) to use their time and resources effectively.

A systematic approach to designing evaluations takes into account the questions guiding the study, the constraints evaluators face in studying the program, and the information needs of the intended users. After exploring program and data issues, the initial evaluation question may need to be revised to ensure it is both appropriate and feasible. Since the rise in agency performance reporting, an enormous amount of program information is available and there are myriad ways to analyze it. By selecting the most appropriate measures carefully and giving attention to the most accurate and reliable ways to collect data on them, evaluators ensure the relevance of the analysis and blunt potential criticisms in advance. Choosing well-regarded criteria against which to make comparisons can lead to strong, defensible conclusions. Carefully thinking through data and analysis choices in advance can enhance the quality, credibility, and usefulness of an evaluation by increasing the strength and specificity of the findings and recommendations. Focusing the evaluation design on answering the questions being asked also will likely improve the usefulness of the product to the intended users.

Giving careful attention to evaluation design choices also saves time and resources. Collecting data through interviews, observation, or analysis of records, and ensuring the quality of those data, can be costly and time consuming for the evaluator as well as those subject to the evaluation. Evaluators should aim to select the least burdensome way to obtain the information necessary to address the evaluation question. When initiated to inform decisions, an evaluation's timeliness is especially important to its usefulness. Evaluation design also involves considering whether a credible evaluation can be conducted in the time and resources available and, if not, what alternative information could be provided.

Developing a written evaluation design helps evaluators agree on and communicate a clear plan of action to the project team and its advisers, requestors, and other stakeholders, and it guides and coordinates the project team's activities as the evaluation proceeds. In addition, a written plan justifying design decisions facilitates documentation of decisions and procedures in the final report.

Five Key Steps to an Evaluation Design

Evaluations are studies tailored to answer specific questions about how well (or whether) a program is working. To ensure that the resulting information and analyses meet decision maker's needs, it is particularly useful to isolate the tasks and choices involved in putting together a good evaluation design. We propose that the following five steps be completed before significant data are collected. These steps give structure to the rest of this publication:

1. Clarify understanding of the program's goals and strategy.

2. Develop relevant and useful evaluation questions.

3. Select an appropriate evaluation approach or design for each evaluation question.

4. Identify data sources and collection procedures to obtain relevant, credible information.

5. Develop plans to analyze the data in ways that allow valid conclusions to be drawn from the evaluation questions.

The chapters in this paper discuss the iterative process of identifying questions important to program stakeholders and exploring data options (chapters 2 and 3) and the variety of research designs and approaches that the evaluator can choose to yield credible, timely answers within resource constraints (chapters 4 and 5). Completing an evaluation will, of course, entail careful data collection and analysis, drawing conclusions against the evaluation criteria selected, and reporting the findings, conclusions, and recommendations, if any. Numerous textbooks on research methods are adequate guides to ensuring valid and reliable data collection and analysis (for example, Rossi et al. 2004, Wholey et al. 2010). GAO analysts are also urged to consult their design and methodology specialists as well as the technical guides available on GAO's Intranet.

How evaluation results are communicated can dramatically affect how they are used. Generally, evaluators should discuss preferred reporting options with the evaluation's requesters to ensure that their expectations are met and prepare a variety of reporting formats (for example, publications and briefings) to meet the needs of the varied audiences that are expected to be interested in the evaluation's results.

GAO-12-208G

For More Information

GAO documents	GAO. 2011. *Performance Measurement and Evaluation: Definitions and Relationships*, GAO-11-646SP. Washington, D.C. May.
	GAO. 1998. *Program Evaluation: Agencies Challenged by New Demand for Information on Program Results*, GAO/GGD-98-53. Washington, D.C. Apr. 24.
	GAO. 2005. *Program Evaluation: OMB's PART Reviews Increased Agencies' Attention to Improving Evidence of Program Results*, GAO-06-67. Washington, D.C. Oct. 28.
	GAO. 2000. Program Evaluation: Studies Helped Agencies Measure or Explain Program Performance, GAO/GGD-00-204. Washington, D.C. Sept. 29.
Other resources	American Evaluation Association. 2010. *An Evaluation Roadmap for a More Effective Government*. www.eval.org/EPTF.asp
	Bernholz, Eric, and others. 2006. *Evaluation Dialogue Between OMB Staff and Federal Evaluators: Digging a Bit Deeper into Evaluation Science*. Washington, D.C. July. http://www.fedeval.net/docs/omb2006briefing.pdf
	OMB (U. S. Office of Management and Budget). 2009. *Increased Emphasis on Program Evaluations*, M-10-01, Memorandum for the Heads of Executive Departments and Agencies. Washington, D.C.The White House, Oct. 7.
	Rossi, Peter H., Mark W. Lipsey, and Howard E. Freeman. 2004. *Evaluation: A Systematic Approach*, 7th ed. Thousand Oaks, Calif.: Sage.
	U.S. Department of Health and Human Services, Administration for Children and Families, Office of Planning, Research and Evaluation. 2010. *The Program Manager's Guide to Evaluation*, 2nd ed. Washington, D.C. http://www.acf.hhs.gov/programs/opre/other_resrch/pm_guide_eval/

Wholey, Joseph S., Harry P. Hatry, and Kathryn E. Newcomer. 2010. *Handbook of Practical Program Evaluation,* 3rd ed. San Francisco, Calif.: Jossey-Bass.

Chapter 2: Defining the Evaluation's Scope

Because an evaluation can take any number of directions, the first steps in its design aim to define its purpose and scope—to establish what questions it will and will not address. The evaluation's scope is tied to its research questions and defines the subject matter it will assess, such as a program or aspect of a program, and the time periods and locations that will be included. To ensure the evaluation's credibility and relevance to its intended users, the evaluator must develop a clear understanding of the program's purpose and goals and develop researchable evaluation questions that are feasible, appropriate to the program and that address the intended users' needs.

Clarify the Program's Goals and Strategy

For some but not all federal programs, the authorizing legislation and implementing regulations outline the program's purpose, scope, and objectives; the need it was intended to address; and who it is intended to benefit. The evaluator should review the policy literature and consult agency officials and other stakeholders to learn how they perceive the program's purpose and goals, the activities and organizations involved, and the changes in scope or goals that may have occurred.[1] It is also important to identify the program's stage of maturity. Is the program still under development, adapting to conditions on the ground, or is it a complete system of activities purposefully directed at achieving agreed-on goals and objectives? A program's maturity affects the evaluator's ability to describe its strategy and anticipate likely evaluation questions.

Evaluators use program logic models—flow diagrams that describe a program's components and desired results—to explain the strategy—or logic—by which the program is expected to achieve its goals. By specifying a theory of program expectations at each step, a logic model or other representation can help evaluators articulate the assumptions and expectations of program managers and stakeholders. In turn, by specifying expectations, a model can help evaluators define measures of the program's performance and progress toward its ultimate goals. (For examples, see GAO 2002.)

At a minimum, a program logic model should outline the program's inputs, activities or processes, outputs, and both short-term and long-term

---

[1]Program stakeholders are those individuals or groups with a significant interest in how well the program functions, for example, decision makers, funders, administrators and staff, and clients or intended beneficiaries.

outcomes—that is, the ultimate social, environmental, or other benefits envisioned. Including short-term and intermediate outcomes helps identify precursors that may be more readily measured than ultimate benefits, which may take years to achieve. It is also important to include any external factors believed to have an important influence on—either to hinder or facilitate—program inputs, operations, or achievement of intended results. External factors can include the job market or other federal or nonfederal activities aimed at the same outcomes. (Figure 1 is a generic logic model developed for agricultural extension programs; more complex models may describe multiple paths or perspectives.)

Figure 1: Sample Program Logic Model

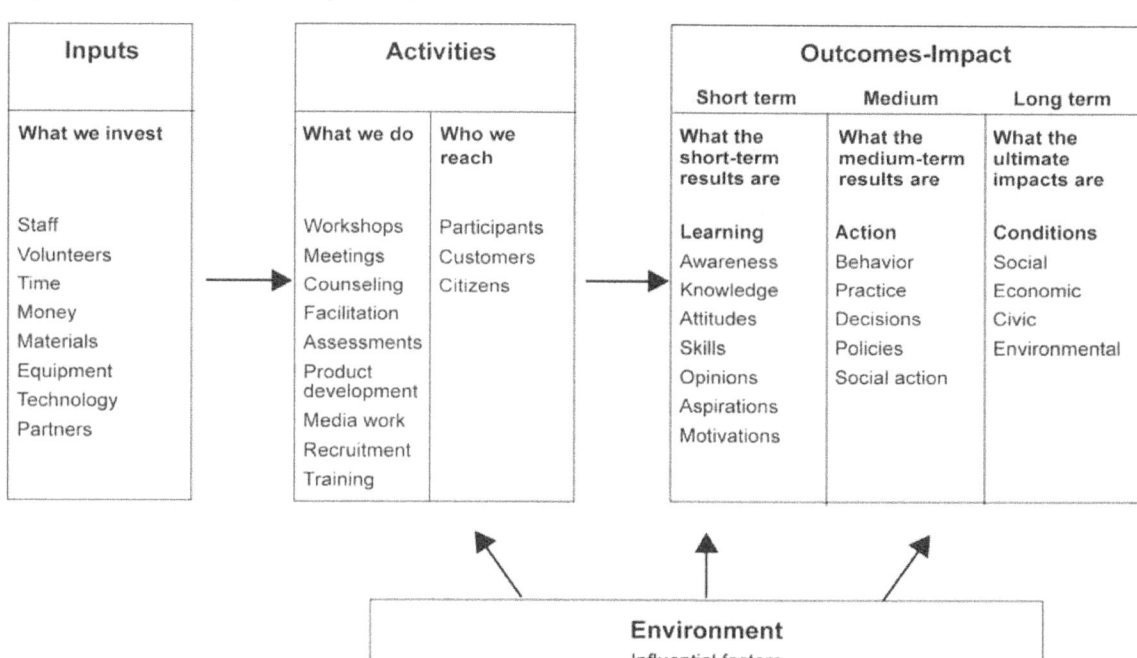

Source: GAO and University of Wisconsin-Extension, Program Development and Evaluation.

A variety of formats can usefully assist in defining the evaluation's scope; the key is to develop a clear understanding of the nature of the program, the context in which it operates, and the policy issues involved. A logic model can be helpful as a:

- program planning tool: (reading from right to left) depicting the implications for program design of previous research on the key factors influencing achievement of the desired benefits;

- communication tool: encouraging shared understanding and expectations among policy makers and program managers and obtaining the support and cooperation of program partners;

- program implementation tool: mapping what activities should occur at various times and which groups should be involved; and

- evaluation tool: helping to define performance measures and formulate evaluation questions.

In describing a program's goals and strategies, it is important to consult a variety of sources—legislative history, program staff and materials, prior research on the program, public media, congressional staff—to uncover (if not resolve) any differences in expectations and concerns program stakeholders have. It is also important to understand the program's policy context, why it was initiated, whether circumstances have changed importantly since its inception, and what the current policy concerns are. In the absence of clearly established definitions of the intervention or its desired outcomes, the evaluator will need to discuss these issues with the requestor and may need to explore, as part of the evaluation, how the program and its goals have been operationally defined (see the discussion of flexible grant programs in chapter 5).

Develop Relevant and Useful Evaluation Questions

Evaluation questions are constructed so that the issues and concerns of a program's stakeholders about program performance can be articulated and to focus the evaluation to help ensure that its findings are useful (GAO 2004). It is important to work with the evaluation requester to formulate the right question to ensure that the completed evaluation will meet his or her information needs. Care should be taken at this step because evaluation questions frame the scope of the assessment and drive the evaluation design—the selection of data to collect and comparisons to make.

Program managers and policy makers may request information about program performance to help them make diverse program management, design, and budgeting decisions. Depending on the program's history and current policy context, the purpose for conducting an evaluation may be to assist program improvement or to provide accountability, or both. More specifically, evaluations may be conducted to

- ascertain the program's progress in implementing key provisions,

- assess the extent of the program's effectiveness in achieving desired outcomes,

- identify effective practices for achieving desired results,

- identify opportunities to improve program performance,

- ascertain the success of corrective actions,

- guide resource allocation within a program, or

- support program budget requests.

These purposes imply different focuses—on the program as a whole or just a component—as well as different evaluation questions and, thus, designs. For example, if the purpose of the evaluation is to guide program resource allocation, then the evaluation question might be tailored to identify which program participants are in greatest need of services, or which program activities are most effective in achieving the desired results. To draw valid conclusions on which practices are most effective in achieving the desired results, the evaluation might examine a few carefully chosen sites in order to directly compare the effects of alternative practices on the same outcomes, under highly comparable conditions. (For further discussion see chapter 4 and GAO 2000.)

To be researchable, evaluation questions should be clear and specific and use terms that can be readily defined and measured, and meet the requester's needs, so that the study's scope and purpose are readily understood and feasible. Evaluation questions should also be objective, fair, and politically neutral; the phrasing of a question should not presume to know the answer in advance.

Clarify the Issue

Congressional requests for evaluations often begin with a very broad concern, so discussion may be necessary to determine the requester's priorities and develop clearly defined researchable questions. Moreover, while potentially hundreds of questions could be asked about a program, limitations on evaluation resources and time require focusing the study on the most important questions that can be feasibly addressed. The evaluator can use the program's logic model to organize the discussion systematically to learn whether the requester's concerns focus on how the program is operating or whether it is achieving its intended results or producing unintended effects (either positive or negative). It is also important to ensure that the evaluation question is well-matched to the program's purpose and strategies. For example, if a program is targeted to meet the housing needs of low-income residents, then it would be inappropriate to judge its effectiveness by whether the housing needs of all residents were met.

It is important to learn whether the requester has a specific set of criteria or expectations in mind to judge the program against and whether questions pertain to the entire program or just certain components. A general request to "assess a program's effectiveness" should be clarified and rephrased as a more specific question that ensures a common understanding of the program's desired outcomes, such as, "Has the program led to increased access to health care for low-income residents?" or "Has it led to lower incidence of health problems for those residents?" It is also important to distinguish questions about the overall effectiveness of a nationwide program from those limited to a few sites that warrant study because they are especially promising or problematic. The difference is extremely important for evaluation scope and design, and attention to the difference allows the evaluator to help make the study useful to the requester.

Although the feasibility of the evaluation questions will continue to be assessed during the design phase, an evaluator should gain agreement on these questions before completing the design of the evaluation. If program stakeholders perceive the questions as objective and reflecting their key concerns, they will be more likely to find the evaluation results credible and persuasive and act on them.

Ensure That Questions Are Appropriate to the Program's Stage of Maturity

Different questions tend to be asked at different stages of program maturity and often reflect whether the purpose of the study is to assist program improvement or provide accountability. Three types of evaluation are defined by whether the focus is on the program's operations or outcomes, or on the program's causal link to the observed results. Of course, a single study may use different approaches to address multiple questions. (See table 1.)

Table 1: Common Evaluation Questions Asked at Different Stages of Program Development

Program stage	Common evaluation questions	Type of evaluation
Early stage of program or new initiative within a program	• Is the program being delivered as intended to the targeted recipients? • Have any feasibility or management problems emerged? • What progress has been made in implementing changes or new provisions?	Process monitoring or process evaluation
Mature, stable program with well-defined program model	• Are desired program outcomes obtained? • What, if any, unintended side effects did the program produce? • Do outcomes differ across program approaches, components, providers, or client subgroups?	Outcome monitoring or outcome evaluation
	• Are program resources being used efficiently? • Why is a program no longer obtaining the desired level of outcomes?	Process evaluation
	• Did the program cause the desired impact? • Is one approach more effective than another in obtaining the desired outcomes?	Net impact evaluation

Source Adapted from Bernholz et al 2006.

Process Evaluations

In the early stages of a new program or initiative within a program, evaluation questions tend to focus on program process—on how well authorized activities are carried out and reach intended recipients. Staff need to be hired and trained, regulations written, buildings leased, materials designed or purchased, participants identified and enrolled. Program managers generally look for quick feedback on whether action is needed to help get the program up and running as intended. Evaluation studies designed to address the quality or efficiency of program operations or their fidelity to program design are frequently called *process or implementation evaluations*. Over time, some of the measures used to evaluate program implementation may be institutionalized into an ongoing program performance monitoring and reporting system. A process evaluation can be an important companion to an outcome or impact evaluation by describing the program as actually experienced.

Outcome Evaluations

Once assured that the program is operating as planned, one may ask whether it is yielding the desired benefits or improvement in outcomes. *Outcome evaluations* assess the extent to which a program achieves its outcome-oriented objectives or other important outcomes. Naturally, if the program has not had sufficient time to get its operations in place, then it is unlikely to have produced the desired benefits. Depending on the nature of the program, this shake-out period might take a few months, a year, or perhaps even longer. In agreeing on an evaluation question, it is also important to consider whether sufficient time will have passed to observe longer-term outcomes. For example, it might take a study 3 or more years to observe whether a program for high school students led to greater success in college.

Net Impact Evaluations

Where a program's desired outcomes are known to also be influenced appreciably by factors outside the program, such as the labor market, the outcomes that are actually observed represent a combination of program effects and the effects of those external factors. In this case, questions about program effectiveness become more sophisticated and the evaluation design should attempt to identify the extent to which the program caused or contributed to those observed changes. *Impact evaluation* is a form of outcome evaluation that assesses the net effect of a program (or its true effectiveness) by comparing the observed outcomes to an estimate of what would have happened in the absence of the program. While outcome measures can be incorporated into ongoing performance monitoring systems, evaluation studies are usually required to assess program net impacts.

For More Information

GAO documents

GAO. 2004. *GAO's Congressional Protocols,* GAO-04-310G. Washington, D.C.: July 16.

GAO. 2000. *Managing for Results: Views on Ensuring the Usefulness of Agency Performance Information to Congress,* GAO/GGD-00-35. Washington, D.C.: Jan. 26.

GAO. 2002. *Program Evaluation: Strategies for Assessing How Information Dissemination Contributes to Agency Goals,* GAO-02-923. Washington, D.C. Sept. 30.

Other resources

Bernholz, Eric, and others. 2006. *Evaluation Dialogue Between OMB Staff and Federal Evaluators: Digging a Bit Deeper into Evaluation Science.* Washington, D.C.: July.
http://www.fedeval.net/docs/omb2006briefing.pdf

Rossi, Peter H., Mark W. Lipsey, and Howard E. Freeman. 2004. *Evaluation: A Systematic Approach,* 7th ed. Thousand Oaks, Calif.: Sage.

University of Wisconsin–Extension, Program Development and Evaluation. www.uwex.edu/ces/pdande/evaluation/evallogicmodel.html

U.S. Department of Health and Human Services, Administration for Children and Families, Office of Planning, Research and Evaluation. 2010. *The Program Manager's Guide to Evaluation*, 2nd ed. Washington, D.C. www.acf.hhs.gov/programs/opre/other_resrch/pm_guide_eval/

Wholey, Joseph S., Harry P. Hatry, and Kathryn E. Newcomer. 2010. *Handbook of Practical Program Evaluation,* 3rd ed. San Francisco: Jossey-Bass.

Chapter 3: The Process of Selecting an Evaluation Design

Once evaluation questions have been formulated, the next step is to develop an evaluation design—to select appropriate measures and comparisons that will permit drawing valid conclusions on those questions. In the design process, the evaluator explores the variety of options available for collecting and analyzing information and chooses alternatives that will best address the evaluation objectives within available resources. Selecting an appropriate and feasible design, however, is an iterative process and may result in the need to revise the evaluation questions.

Key Components of an Evaluation Design

An evaluation design documents the activities best able to provide credible evidence on the evaluation questions within the time and resources available and the logical basis for drawing strong conclusions on those questions. The basic components of an evaluation design include the following:

- the evaluation questions, objectives, and scope;

- information sources and measures, or what information is needed;

- data collection methods, including any sampling procedures, or how information or evidence will be obtained;

- an analysis plan, including evaluative criteria or comparisons, or how or on what basis program performance will be judged or evaluated;

- an assessment of study limitations.

Clearly articulating the evaluation design and its rationale in advance aids in discussing these choices with the requester and other stakeholders. Documenting the study's decisions and assumptions helps manage the study and assists report writing and interpreting results.

GAO's Design Matrix

GAO evaluators outline the components of the evaluation design, as well as the limitations of those choices, in a standard tool called a design matrix. GAO evaluators are expected to complete a design matrix for each significant project to document their decisions and summarize the key issues in the evaluation design. All staff having significant involvement in or oversight of the work meet to discuss this plan and reach agreement on whether it can credibly answer the evaluation questions.

As a government oversight agency that conducts both audits and
evaluations, GAO also uses the design matrix to document and ensure
compliance with the government auditing fieldwork standards for
conducting performance audits (including program evaluations). The
fieldwork standards relate to planning, conducting, and documenting the
study. Government auditors are also expected to document in their plans
the implications of the agency's internal controls, the results of previous
studies, and the reliability of agency databases for the evaluation's scope
and objectives (GAO 2011).

The guidance for GAO's design matrix is shown in figure 2 to
demonstrate the issues, design choices, and trade-offs that an evaluator
is expected to consider. Because GAO addresses a wide variety of
information requests in addition to program evaluations, the guidance is
fairly general but focuses on asking the evaluator to justify the design
components for each researchable question. Finally, the tool can help
stakeholders understand the logic of the evaluation.

Figure 2: Questions Guiding the Selection of Design Components

Researchable Question(s)	Information Required and Source(s)	Scope and Methodology	Limitations	What This Analysis Will Likely Allow GAO to Say
What questions is the team trying to answer? Identify specific questions that the team must ask to address the objectives in the commitment letter and job commitment report. Ensure each major evaluation question is specific, objective, neutral, measurable, and doable. Ensure key terms are defined. Each major evaluation question should be addressed in a separate row.	**What information does the team need to address each evaluation question? Where will they get it?** Identify documents or types of information that the team must have. Identify plans to address internal controls and compliance. Identify plans to collect documents that establish the "criteria" to be used. Identify plans to follow up on known significant findings and open recommendations that team found in obtaining background information. Identify sources of the required information, such as databases, studies, subject area experts, program officials, models, etc.	**How will the team answer each evaluation question?** Describe strategies for collecting the required information or data, such as random sampling, case studies, focus groups, questionnaires, benchmarking to best practices, use of existing data bases, etc. Describe the planned scope of each strategy, including the timeframe, locations to visit, and sample sizes. Describe the analytical techniques to be used, such as regression analysis, cost benefit analysis, sensitivity analysis, modeling, descriptive analysis, content analysis, case study summaries, etc.	**What are the design's limitations and how will it affect the product?** Cite any limitations as a result of the information required or the scope and methodology, such as: —Questionable data quality and/or reliability. —Inability to access certain types of data or obtain data covering a certain time frame. —Security classification or confidentiality restrictions. —Inability to generalize or extrapolate findings to the universe. Be sure to address how these limitations will affect the product.	**What are the expected results of the work?** Describe what GAO can likely say. Draw on preliminary results for illustrative purposes, if helpful. Ensure that the proposed answer addresses the evaluation question in column one.

Source: GAO.

An Iterative Process

Designing an evaluation plan is iterative: evaluation objectives, scope, and methodology are defined together because what determines them often overlaps. Data limitations or new information about the program may arise as work is conducted and have implications for the adequacy of the original plans or the feasibility of answering the original questions. For example, a review of existing studies of alternative program approaches may uncover too few credible evaluations to support conclusions about which approach is most effective. Thus, evaluators should consider the need to make adjustments to the evaluation objectives, scope, and methodology throughout the project.

Nevertheless, the design phase of an evaluation is a period for examining options for answering the evaluation questions and for considering which options offer the strongest approach, given the time and resources available. After reviewing materials about the program, evaluators should develop and compare alternative designs and assess their strengths and weaknesses. For example, in choosing between using program administrative data or conducting a new survey of program officials, the evaluator might consider whether 1) the new information collected through a survey would justify the extra effort required, or 2) a high quality survey can be conducted in the time available.

Collect Background Information

A key first step in designing an evaluation is to conduct a literature review in order to understand the program's history, related policies, and knowledge base. A review of the relevant policy literature can help focus evaluation questions on knowledge gaps, identify design and data collection options used in the past, and provide important context for the requester's questions. An agency's strategic plan and annual performance reports can also provide useful information on available data sources and measures and the efforts made to verify and validate those data (GAO 1998).

Discussing evaluation plans with agency as well as congressional stakeholders is important throughout the design process, since they have a direct interest in and ability to act on the study's findings. A principle of good planning that helps ensure the transparency of our work is to notify agency stakeholders of the evaluation's scope and objectives at its outset and discuss the expected terms of the work (GAO 2004). GAO evaluators also coordinate their work with the Inspector General of the agency whose program is being evaluated, and our sister congressional agencies—the Congressional Budget Office and Congressional Research Service—to avoid duplication, to leverage our resources, and to build a mutual knowledge base. These meetings give evaluators opportunity to learn about previous or ongoing studies and unfolding events that could influence the design and use of the evaluation or necessitate modifying the original evaluation question.

Consider Conducting an Evaluation Synthesis

When a literature review reveals that several previous studies have addressed the evaluation question, then the evaluator should consider conducting a synthesis of their results before collecting new data. An evaluation synthesis can answer questions about overall program effectiveness or whether specific features of the program are working especially well or especially poorly. Findings supported by a number of soundly designed and executed studies add strength to the knowledge base exceeding that of any single study, especially when the findings are consistent across studies that used different methods. If, however, the studies produced inconsistent findings, systematic analysis of the circumstances and methods used across a number of soundly designed and executed studies may provide clues to explain variations in program performance (GAO 1992b). For example, differences between communities in how they staff or execute a program or in their client populations may explain differences in their effectiveness.

A variety of statistical approaches have been proposed for statistically cumulating the results of several studies. A widely used procedure for answering questions about program impacts is "meta-analysis," which is a way of analyzing "effect sizes" across several studies. Effect size is a measure of the difference in outcome between a treatment group and a comparison group. (For more information, see Lipsey and Wilson 2000.)

Assess the Relevance and Quality of Available Data Sources

Depending on the program and study question, potential sources for evidence on the evaluation question include program administrative records, grantee reports, performance monitoring data, surveys of program participants, and existing surveys of the national population or private or public facilities. In addition, the evaluator may choose to conduct independent observations or interviews with public officials, program participants, or persons or organizations doing business with public agencies.

In selecting sources of evidence to answer the evaluation question, the evaluator must assess whether these sources will provide evidence that is both sufficient and appropriate to support findings and conclusions on the evaluation question. Sufficiency refers to the quantity of evidence— whether it is enough to persuade a knowledgeable person that the findings are reasonable. Appropriateness refers to the relevance, validity, and reliability of the evidence in supporting the evaluation objectives. The level of effort required to ensure that computer-processed data (such as agency records) are sufficiently reliable for use will depend on the extent to which the data will be used to support findings and conclusions and the level of risk or sensitivity associated with the study. (See GAO 2009 for more detailed guidance on testing the reliability of computer-processed data.)

Measures are the concrete, observable events or conditions (or units of evidence) that represent the aspects of program performance of interest. Some evaluation questions may specify objective, quantifiable measures, such as the number of families receiving program benefits, or qualitative measures, such as the reasons for noncompliance. But often the evaluator will need to select measures to represent a broader characteristic, such as "service quality." It is important to select measures that clearly represent or are related to the performance they are trying to assess. For example, a measure of the average processing time for tax returns does not represent, and is not clearly related to, the goal of increasing the accuracy of tax return processing. Measures are most usefully selected in concert with the criteria that program performance will be assessed against, so that agreement can be reached on the sufficiency and appropriateness of the evidence for drawing conclusions on those criteria.

Additional considerations for assessing the appropriateness of existing databases include: whether certain subgroups of the population are well-represented; whether converting data from its original format will require excessive time or effort; and when examining multiple sites, whether variation in data across sites precludes making reliable comparisons. No data source is perfectly accurate and reliable; thus, evaluators often consider using multiple measures or sources of data to triangulate toward the truth. Concerns about biases in one data source—for example, possible exaggerations in self reports of employment history— might be countered by complementing that information with similar measures from another source—for example, length of employment recorded in administrative records.

Plan Original Data Collection

No matter how data are collected, care should be taken to ensure that data are sufficient and appropriate to support findings on the evaluation question. Trained observers may inspect physical conditions, actions or records to ascertain whether these met requirements or other kinds of criteria, When collecting testimonial evidence through interviews or surveys, the evaluator should consider whether the people serving as data sources are sufficiently knowledgeable and whether their reports of events or their opinions are likely to be candid and accurate. In addition, careful attention to developing and pretesting questionnaire surveys and other data collection instruments will help ensure that the data obtained are sufficiently accurate for the purposes of the study. Where the evaluator aims to aggregate and generalize from the results of a sample survey, great importance is attached to collecting uniform data from every unit in the sample. Consequently, sample survey information is usually acquired through structured interviews or self-administered questionnaires. Most of the information is collected in close-ended form, which means that the respondent chooses from responses offered in the questionnaire or by the interviewer. Designing a consistent set of responses into the data collection process helps establish the uniformity of data across units in the sample. (For more on designing and conducting surveys, see GAO 1991, Dillman 2007, Fowler 2009, or Willis 2005.)

A qualified survey specialist should be involved in designing and executing questionnaire surveys that will be relied on for evidence on the evaluation questions, whether the surveys are administered in person, by telephone or mail, or over the Internet. Survey specialists can help ensure that surveys are clearly understood, are quick and easy to complete, and obtain the desired information. Subject matter experts should review the survey to assess whether technical terms are used properly, respondents are likely to have the desired information and will be motivated to respond, and the questionnaire will provide a comprehensive, unbiased assessment of the issues.

Federal executive agencies must adhere to guidance that OMB's Office of Information and Regulatory Affairs issues on policies and practices for planning, implementing, and maintaining statistical activities, including surveys used in program evaluations (OMB 2006). In addition, executive branch agencies must submit certain proposals to collect information from the public for OMB's review and approval to ensure that they meet the requirements of the Paperwork Reduction Act. GAO, as a legislative branch agency, is not subject to these policies.

A potentially less costly alternative to conducting an original survey (especially one with a large national sample) is to pay for additional questions to be added to an ongoing national survey. This "piggy-back" strategy is only useful, of course, if that survey samples the same population needed for the evaluation. Another useful alternative data collection approach is to link data from sample surveys to administrative data systems, enabling the evaluator to obtain new information on, for example, individuals, their neighborhoods, or their program participation. (For more on record linkage and privacy protection procedures, see GAO 2001.)

Select Evaluative Criteria

Evaluative criteria are the standards, measures, or expectations about what should exist against which measures of actual performance are compared and evaluated. Evaluators should select evaluative criteria that are relevant, appropriate and sufficient to address the evaluation's objectives. Unlike financial or performance audits, the objectives of program evaluations generally are not to assess a program's or agency's compliance with legal requirements but to assess whether program expectations have been met. The sources of those expectations can be quite diverse. However, if the intended audience for the report—both the study requesters and program managers—believes that the chosen criteria and measures are appropriate, then the study's findings are more likely to be credible.

Depending on the circumstances of the program and the evaluation questions, examples of possible criteria include

- purpose or goals prescribed by law or regulation,

- policies or procedures established by agency officials,

- professional standards or norms,

- expert opinions,

- prior period's performance,

- performance of other entities or sectors used to benchmark performance.

Some criteria designate a particular level as distinguishing acceptable from unacceptable performance, such as in determinations of legal compliance. Related evaluation questions ask whether a program's performance is "acceptable" or "meets expectations." Other criteria have no preestablished level designated as representing acceptable performance but permit assessment of the extent to which expectations are met. Thus, while the evaluation cannot typically ascertain whether a program was "effective" per se, it can compare the performance of a program across time and to the performance of other programs or organizations to ascertain whether it is more or less effective than other efforts to achieve a given objective.

To support objective assessment, criteria must be observable and measurable events, actions, or characteristics that provide evidence that performance objectives have been met. Some legislation, evaluation requests, or program designs provide broad concepts for performance objectives, such as "a thorough process" or "family well-being," that lack clear assessment criteria. In such cases, the evaluator may need to gain the agreement of study requesters and program managers to base assessment criteria on measures and standards in the subject matter literature.

Select a Sample of Observations

In some cases, it makes sense to include all members of a population in a study, especially where the population is small enough that it is feasible within available resources and time periods to collect and analyze data on the entire population (such as the 50 states)—called a certainty sample or census. Many federal programs, however, cannot be studied by means of a census and the evaluator must decide whether to collect data on a probability or nonprobability sample.

In a probability sample (sometimes referred to as a statistical or random sample), each unit in the population has a known, nonzero chance of being selected. The results of a probability sample can usually be generalized to the population from which the sample was taken. If the objective is to report characteristics about a population, such as the percentage of an agency's officials who received certain training, or the total dollar value of transactions in error in an agency's system, then a probability sample may be appropriate. A sampling specialist can help identify how large a sample is needed to obtain precise estimates or detect expected effects of a given size.

In a nonprobability sample, some units in the population have no chance, or an unknown chance, of being selected. In nonprobability sampling, a sample is selected from knowledge of the population's characteristics or from a subset of a population. Selecting locations to visit and identifying officials to interview are part of many GAO studies, and these choices are usually made using a nonprobability sampling approach. However, if it is important to avoid the appearance of selection bias, locations or interviewees can be selected using random sampling.

Deciding whether to use probability sampling is a key element of the study design that flows from the scope of the researchable question. If the question is, What progress has been made in implementing new program provisions? then the implied study scope is program-wide and a probability sample would be required to generalize conclusions drawn from the locations observed to the program as a whole. In contrast, a question about why a program is no longer obtaining the desired level of outcomes might be addressed by following up program locations that have already been identified as not meeting the expected level of outcomes—a purposive, nonprobability sample. A sampling specialist should help select and design a sampling approach. (For more on sampling, see GAO 1992a, Henry 1990, Lohr 2010, or Scheaffer et al. 2006.)

Pilot Test Data Collection and Analysis Procedures

When engaging in primary (or original) data collection, it is important to conduct a pretest or pilot study before beginning full-scale data collection. The pilot study gives the evaluator an opportunity to refine the design and test the availability, reliability, and appropriateness of proposed data. Evaluators new to the program or proposing new data collection may find that a limited exploration of the proposed design in a few sites can provide a useful "reality check" on whether one's assumptions hold true. The pilot phase allows for a check on whether program operations, such as client recruitment, and delivery of services occur as expected. Finding that they do not may suggest a need to refocus the evaluation question to ask why the program has been implemented so differently from what was proposed. Testing the work at one or more sites allows the evaluator to confirm that data are available, the form they take, and the means for gathering them, including interview procedures. It also provides an opportunity to assess whether the analysis methodology will be appropriate.

Existing data sources should be closely examined for their suitability for the planned analyses. For example, to support sophisticated statistical analyses, data may be needed as actual dollars, days, or hours rather than aggregated into a few wide ranges. To ensure the ability to reliably assess change over time, the evaluator should check whether there have been changes in data recording, coding, or storage procedures over the period of interest.

Assess Study Limitations

Evaluators need to work with the stakeholders and acknowledge what the study can and cannot address when making the project's scope and design final. The end of the design phase is an important milestone. It is here that the evaluator must have a clear understanding of what has been chosen, what has been omitted, what strengths and weaknesses have been embedded in the design, what the customer's needs are, how usefully the design is likely to meet those needs, and whether the constraints of time, cost, staff, location, and facilities have been adequately addressed. Evaluators must be explicit about the limitations of the study. They should ask, How conclusive is the study likely to be, given the design? How detailed are the data collection and data analysis plans? What trade-offs were made in developing these plans?

Criteria for a Good Design

GAO and other organizations have developed guidelines or standards to help ensure the quality, credibility, and usefulness of evaluations. (See appendix I and the guidance in GAO's design matrix, figure 2, as an example.) Some standards pertain specifically to the evaluator's organization (for example, whether a government auditor is independent), the planning process (for example, whether stakeholders were consulted), or reporting (for example, documenting assumptions and procedures). While the underlying principles substantially overlap, the evaluator will need to determine the relevance of each guideline to the evaluator's organizational affiliation and their specific evaluation's scope and purpose.

Strong evaluations employ methods of analysis that are appropriate to the question; support the answer with sufficient and appropriate evidence; document the assumptions, procedures, and modes of analysis; and rule out competing explanations. Strong studies present questions clearly, address them appropriately, and draw inferences commensurate with the power of the design and the availability, validity, and reliability of the data. Thus, a good evaluation design should

- be appropriate for the evaluation questions and context. The design should address all key questions, clearly state any limitations in scope, and be appropriate to the nature and significance of the program or issue. For example, evaluations should not attempt to measure outcomes before a program has been in place long enough to be able to produce them.

- adequately address the evaluation question. The strength of the design should match the precision, completeness, and conclusiveness of the information needed to answer the questions and meet the client's needs. Criteria and measures should be narrowly tailored, and comparisons should be selected to support valid conclusions and rule out alternative explanations.

- fit available time and resources. Time and cost are constraints that shape the scope of the evaluation questions and the range of activities that can help answer them. Producing information with an understanding of the user's timetable enhances its usefulness.

- rely on sufficient, credible data. No data collection and maintenance process is free of error, but the data should be sufficiently free of bias or other significant errors that could lead to inaccurate conclusions. Measures should reflect the persons, activities, or conditions that the program is expected to affect and should not be unduly influenced by factors outside the program's control.

For More Information

On sampling approaches	GAO. 1992a. *Using Statistical Sampling*, revised, GAO/PEMD-10.1.6. Washington, D.C. May.
	Henry, Gary T. 1990. *Practical Sampling.* Thousand Oaks, Calif.: Sage.
	Lohr, Sharon L. 2010. *Sampling: Design and Analysis*, 2nd ed. Brooks/Cole, Cengage Learning.
	Scheaffer, Richard L., William Mendenhall III, and R. Lyman Ott. 2006. *Elementary Survey Sampling*, 6th ed. Cengage Learning.
On developing surveys and questionnaires	Dillman, Don A. 2007. *Mail and Internet Surveys: The Tailored Design Method,* 2nd ed. New York: Wiley.
	Fowler, Floyd J., Jr. 2009. *Survey Research Methods*, 4h ed. Thousand Oaks, Calif.: Sage.
	GAO. 1991. *Using Structured Interviewing Techniques.* GAO/PEMD-10.1.5. Washington, D.C. June.
	Willis, Gordon B. 2005. *Cognitive Interviewing: A Tool for Improving Questionnaire Design.* Thousand Oaks, Calif.: Sage.
On standards	American Evaluation Association. 2004. *Guiding Principles for Evaluators.* July. www.eval.org/Publications/GuidingPrinciples.asp.

GAO. 2011. *Government Auditing Standards: 2011 Internet Version.* Washington, D.C. August. http://www.gao.gov/govaud/iv2011gagas.pdf

GAO. 1992b. *The Evaluation Synthesis*, revised, GAO/PEMD-10.1.2. Washington, D.C. March.

Yarbrough, Donald B., Lynn M. Shulha, Rodney K. Hopson, and Flora A. Caruthers. 2011. *The Program Evaluation Standards: A Guide for Evaluators and Evaluation Users*, 3rd ed. Thousand Oaks, Calif.: Sage.

Other resources

GAO. 2009. *Assessing the Reliability of Computer-Processed Data*, external version 1. GAO-09-680G. Washington, D.C. July.

GAO. 2004. *GAO's Agency Protocols,* GAO-05-35G. Washington, D.C. October.

GAO. 2001. *Record Linkage and Privacy: Issues in Creating New Federal Research and Statistical Information.* GAO-01-126SP. Washington, D.C. April.

GAO. 1998. *The Results Act: An Evaluator's Guide to Assessing Agency Annual Performance Plans*, version 1. GAO/GGD-10.1.20. Washington, D.C. April.

Lipsey, Mark W., and David R. Wilson. 2000. *Practical Meta-Analysis.* Thousand Oaks, Calif.: Sage.

OMB (U.S. Office of Management and Budget), Office of Information and Regulatory Affairs. 2006. *Standards and Guidelines for Statistical Surveys.* Washington, D.C. September.
http://www.whitehouse.gov/omb/inforeg_statpolicy#pr

Chapter 4: Designs for Assessing Program Implementation and Effectiveness

Program evaluation designs are tailored to the nature of the program and the questions being asked. Thus, they can have an infinite variety of forms as evaluators choose performance goals and measures and select procedures for data collection and analysis. Nevertheless, individual designs tend to be adaptations of a set of familiar evaluation approaches—that is, evaluation questions and research methods for answering them (Rossi et al. 2004). This chapter provides examples of some typical evaluation approaches for implementation and effectiveness questions and examples of designs specifically matched to program structure. Chapter 5 provides examples of approaches to evaluating programs where either the intervention or desired outcomes are not clearly defined.

Typical Designs for Implementation Evaluations

Implementation (or process) evaluations address questions about how and to what extent activities have been implemented as intended and whether they are targeted to appropriate populations or problems. Implementation evaluations are very similar to performance monitoring in assessing the quality and efficiency of program operations, service delivery, and service use, except that they are conducted as separate projects, not integrated into the program's daily routine. Implementation evaluations may be conducted to provide feedback to program managers, accountability to program sponsors and the public, or insight into variation in program outcomes. These evaluations may answer questions such as

- Are mandated or authorized activities being carried out?

- To what extent is the program reaching the intended population?

- Have feasibility or management problems emerged?

- Why is the program no longer achieving its expected outcomes?

Assessing how *well* a program is operating requires first identifying a criterion against which a program's performance is compared. Alternatively, an assessment may compare performance across locations, points in time, or subgroups of the population, to identify important variations in performance. In contrast, an *exploratory case study* of program processes and context may focus on exploring reasons why the program is operating as it is. Table 2 provides examples of implementation questions and designs used to address them.

Table 2: Common Designs for Implementation (or Process) Evaluations

Evaluation question	Design
Is the program being implemented as intended?	Compare program activities to statute and regulations, program logic model, professional standards, or stakeholder expectations
Have any feasibility or management problems emerged?	• Compare program performance to quality, cost or efficiency expectations • Assess variation in quality or performance across settings, providers, or subgroups of recipients
Why is the program not (or no longer) achieving expected outcomes?	• Analyze program and external factors correlated with variation in program outcomes • Interview key informants about possible explanations • Conduct indepth analysis of critical cases

Source GAO.

Assessing Quality or the Progress of Program Implementation

Assessments of program implementation often compare program performance—or *what is*—to a criterion established in advance—or *what should be*. The evaluative criteria may be derived from the law, regulations, a program logic model, administrative or professional standards, research identifying the best practices of leading organizations, or stakeholder expectations. Some criteria identify an acceptable level of performance or performance standard by, for example, defining authorized activities. In some areas, a program may not be considered credible unless it meets well-established professional standards. When criteria have no predetermined standard of acceptable performance, the evaluator's task is to measure the extent to which a program meets its objectives. Measures of program performance may be obtained from program records or may be specially collected for the evaluation through interviews, observations, or systems testing. For example,

- To assess the quality, objectivity, utility, and integrity of an agency's statistical program, an evaluator can compare its policies and procedures for designing, collecting, processing, analyzing and disseminating data with government guidelines for conducting statistical surveys (OMB 2006).

- To evaluate the operational quality and efficiency of a program providing financial assistance to individuals, an evaluator might analyze administrative records that document the applications received for program benefits and the actions taken on them. Efficiency might be assessed by how promptly applications for benefits were processed for a given level of staffing; quality might be

assessed by how accurately eligibility and benefits were determined
(GAO 2010). Standards of acceptable or desired performance might
be drawn from previous experience or the levels of quality assurance
achieved in other financial assistance programs.

- To evaluate a program's success in serving a target population such
  as low-income children, one might analyze program records to
  compare the family incomes of current participants to the national
  poverty level or to family income levels of recipients in previous years.
  However, to address how well the program is reaching the population
  eligible for the program, a better choice might be to compare
  information from local program records with surveys of the income of
  local residents to estimate the proportion of the local low-income
  population that the program reached. To assess improvement in
  program targeting, the evaluator could compare that program
  coverage statistic over time. However, additional analysis would be
  required to ascertain whether observed improvements in coverage
  resulted from program improvements or changes in the neighborhood.

Assessing Variation in Implementation

To identify program management or feasibility issues in federal programs,
it is often important to examine the nature and sources of variation in
program quality or performance across settings, providers, or population
subgroups. For example,

- To evaluate how well a new technical assistance program is
  operating, an evaluator might review program records as well as
  survey local program managers to learn whether any feasibility
  problems had developed. Program records might address whether
  guidance materials were issued and delivered in a timely manner or
  whether workshops were held promptly and drew the attendance
  expected. But an evaluator might also want to survey local managers
  for their judgments on whether the guidance and training materials
  were technically competent and relevant to their needs. Performance
  standards might be drawn from program design and planning
  materials, program technical standards, or previous experience with
  needs for technical assistance.

Because of the cost of collecting and analyzing data on all program
participants or transactions, evaluators of federal programs frequently
collect data by surveying a nationally representative probability sample.
Sample surveys can also address questions about variation in service
delivery across geographic locations or types of providers.

Case Studies

In some circumstances, an evaluator may want to use case studies to explore certain issues in more depth than can be done in more than a few locations. In single case study evaluations, especially, much attention is given to acquiring qualitative information that describes events and conditions from several points of view. The structure imposed on the data collection may range from the flexibility of ethnography or investigative reporting to the highly structured interviews of sample surveys. (For more on the evaluation insights to be gained from ethnography, see GAO 2003.) Case studies are often used to provide in-depth *descriptive* information about how the program operates in the field. If the objective of the case study is to describe aspects of an issue, provide context, or illustrate findings developed from a more broadly applied survey, then selecting a nongeneralizable sample of cases may be appropriate.

Case studies can also supplement survey or administrative data to explore specific questions about program performance, such as understanding variation in program performance across locations (for example, rural versus urban settings), or to identify factors key to program success or failure. The criteria used for selecting cases are critical to one's ability to apply their findings to the larger program. To heighten the value of the information they provide, cases should be selected carefully to represent particular conditions of interest (for example, sites with low versus high levels of performance) and with certain hypotheses in mind. However, most often, case studies will generate hypotheses rather than answers to questions such as what factors influence program success. (For more on case study methodology, see GAO 1990, Stake 1995, or Yin 2009.) For example,

- To identify the causes of a sudden decline in control of an agricultural pest, evaluators might conduct field observations in the localities most affected to assess how well key components of the pest eradication and control program were executed or whether some other factor appeared to be responsible.

Typical Designs for Outcome Evaluations

Outcome evaluations address questions about the extent to which the program achieved its results-oriented objectives. This form of evaluation focuses on examining outputs (goods and services delivered by a program) and outcomes (the results of those products and services) but may also assess program processes to understand how those outcomes are produced. Outcome evaluations may address questions such as

- Is the program achieving its intended purposes or objectives?

- Has it had other important (unintended) side effects on issues of stakeholder concern?

- Do outcomes differ across program approaches, components, providers, or client subgroups?

- How does the program compare with other strategies for achieving the same ends?

To appropriately assess *program effectiveness*, it is important, first, to select outcome measures that clearly represent the nature of the expected program benefit, cover key aspects of desired performance, and are not unduly influenced by factors outside the program's control. Next, to allow causal inferences about program effects, the data collection and analysis plan must establish a correlation between exposure to the program and the desired benefit and must set a time-order relationship such that program exposure precedes outcomes.

However, if the evaluators suspect that factors outside the program appreciably influenced the observed outcomes, then they should not present the findings of an outcome evaluation as representing the results caused by the program. Instead, they should choose one of the net impact designs discussed in the next section to attempt to isolate effects attributable to the program. Ongoing monitoring of social conditions such as a community's health or employment status can provide valuable feedback to program managers and the public about progress toward program goals but may not directly reflect program performance. Table 3 provides examples of outcome-oriented evaluation questions and designs used to address them.

Table 3: Common Designs for Outcome Evaluations

Evaluation question	Design
Is the program achieving its desired outcomes or having other important side effects?	• Compare program performance to law and regulations, program logic model, professional standards, or stakeholder expectations • Assess change in outcomes for participants before and after exposure to the program • Assess differences in outcomes between program participants and nonparticipants
Do program outcomes differ across program components, providers or recipients?	Assess variation in outcomes (or change in outcomes) across approaches, settings, providers, or subgroups of recipients

Source GAO.

Assessing the Achievement of Intended Outcomes

Like outcome monitoring, outcome evaluations often assess the benefits of the program for participants or the broader public by comparing data on program outcomes to a preestablished target value. The criterion could be derived from law, regulation, or program design, while the target value might be drawn from professional standards, stakeholder expectations, or the levels observed previously in this or similar programs. This can help ensure that target levels for accomplishments, compliance, or absence of error are realistic. For example,

- To assess the immediate outcomes of instructional programs, an evaluator could measure whether participants' experienced short-term changes in knowledge, attitudes, or skills at the end of their training session. The evaluator might employ post-workshop surveys or conduct observations during the workshops to document how well participants understood and can use what was taught. Depending on the topic, industry standards might provide a criterion of 80 percent or 90 percent accuracy, or demonstration of a set of critical skills, to define program success. Although observational data may be considered more accurate indicators of knowledge and skill gains than self-report surveys, they can often be more resource-intensive to collect and analyze.

Assessing Change in Outcomes

In programs where there are quantitative measures of performance but no established standard or target value, outcome evaluations at least may rely on assessing *change or differences* in desired outputs and outcomes. The level of the outcome of interest, such as client behavior or environmental conditions, is compared with the level observed in the absence of the program or intervention. This can be done by comparing

- the behavior of individuals before and after their exposure to a program,

- environmental conditions before and after an intervention, or

- the outcomes for individuals who did and did not participate in the program.

Of course, to conclude that any changes observed reflect program effects, the evaluator must feel confident that those changes would not have occurred on their own without the program, in response to some nonprogram influences. For example,

- The accuracy and timeliness of severe weather forecasts—arguably considered program *outputs*—can be compared to target levels of performance through analysis of program records over time. However, it is more problematic to attempt to assess the *effectiveness* of the forecasting program through the amount of harm resulting from those storms—what might be considered program outcomes. This is because building construction and evacuation policies—external factors to a weather forecasting program—are also expected to greatly influence the amount of harm produced by a storm.

- To assess an industry's compliance with specific workplace safety regulations, an evaluator could conduct work-site observations or review agency inspections records and employer injury and illness reports. The evaluator might analyze changes in compliance and safety levels at work sites after a regulation was enacted or compare compliance and safety levels between employers who were or were not provided assistance in complying with the regulations. Again, however, to draw conclusions about the *effectiveness or impact* of the regulation (or compliance assistance) in improving worker safety, the evaluator needs to be able to rule out the influence of other possible workplace changes, such as in technology, worker experience, or other aspects of working conditions.

As in process evaluations, sample surveys can be used to collect outcome data on probability samples in order to provide information about the program as a whole. A cross-sectional survey, the simplest form of sample survey, takes measurements at a point in time to describe events or conditions. By providing information on the incidence of events or distribution of conditions in relationship to a preselected standard or target value, it can be used to assess program performance in either a process or an outcome evaluation. Through repeated application, a cross-sectional survey can measure change over time for the *population* as a *whole*. A *panel survey* acquires information from the same sample units at two or more points in time. Thus, a panel survey can provide less variable measures of *change* in facts, attitudes, or opinions over time and thus can support more directly comparative assessments of outcomes than can a cross-sectional survey, although often at greater cost. Adding the important element of time helps in drawing inferences with regard to cause and effect.

Assessing Variation in Outcomes

Variation in outcomes across settings, providers or populations can be the result of variation in program operations (such as level of enforcement) or context (such as characteristics of client populations or settings). Variation in outcomes associated with features under program control, such as the characteristics of service providers or their activities, may identify opportunities for managers to take action to improve performance. However, additional information is usually needed to understand why some providers are obtaining worse results than others—for example, whether the staff lack needed skills or are ineffectively managed. Variation associated with factors outside the control of the program, such as neighborhood characteristics, can help explain program results, but may not identify actions to improve program performance. Thus, although analysis of surveys or performance reports can identify factors *correlated* with variation in outcomes, follow-up studies or more complex designs (see the next section) are needed to draw firm conclusions about their likely causes.

Case studies are not usually used to assess program effectiveness because their results cannot be generalized to the program as a whole and because of the difficulty of distinguishing many possible causes of a unique instance. However, in special circumstances, an outcome evaluation may use a case study to examine a *critical instance* closely to understand its cause or consequences. Often such a study is an investigation of a specific problem event, such as a fatal accident or forest fire. The potential causal factors can be numerous and complex, requiring an in-depth examination to assess whether and which safety program components were ineffective in preventing or responding to that event. Critical incident studies are also discussed in chapter 5.

Typical Designs for Drawing Causal Inferences about Program Impacts

Many desired outcomes of federal programs are influenced by external factors, including other federal, state, and local programs and policies, as well as economic or environmental conditions. Thus, the outcomes observed typically reflect a combination of influences. To isolate the program's unique impacts, or contribution to those outcomes, an impact study must be carefully designed to rule out plausible alternative explanations for the results. Typical approaches to this problem include

- selection of targeted outcome measures,

- comparison group research designs,

- statistical analysis, and

- logical argument.

A well-articulated program logic model is quite valuable in planning an impact evaluation. Clearly articulating the program's strategy and performance expectations aids the selection of appropriate performance measures and data sources. Identifying the most important external influences on desired program outcomes helps in developing research designs that convincingly rule out the most plausible alternative explanations for the observed results.

Impact evaluation research designs construct comparisons of what happened after exposure to the program with an estimate of what would have happened in the absence of the program in order to estimate the net impact of the program. A number of methodologies are available to estimate program impact, including experimental, quasi-experimental, and nonexperimental designs. Conducting an impact evaluation of a social intervention often requires the expenditure of significant resources to collect and analyze data on program results and estimate what would have happened in the absence of the program. Thus, impact evaluations need not be conducted for all interventions but should be reserved for when the effort and cost appear warranted: for an intervention that is important, clearly defined, well-implemented, and being considered for adoption elsewhere (GAO 2009). Table 4 provides examples of designs commonly used to address net impact questions.

Table 4: Common Designs for Drawing Causal Inferences about Program Impacts

Evaluation question	Design
Is the program responsible for (effective in) achieving improvements in desired outcomes?	• Compare (change in) outcomes for a randomly assigned treatment group and a nonparticipating control group (*randomized controlled experiment*)
	• Compare (change in) outcomes for program participants and a comparison group closely matched to them on key characteristics (*comparison group quasi-experiment*)
	• Compare (change in) outcomes for participants before and after the intervention, over multiple points in time with statistical controls (*single group quasi-experiment*)
How does the effectiveness of the program approach compare with other strategies for achieving the same outcomes?	• Compare (change in) outcomes for groups randomly assigned to different treatments (*randomized controlled experiment*)
	• Compare (change in) outcomes for comparison groups closely matched on key characteristics (*comparison group quasi-experiment*)

Source Adapted from Bernholz et al 2006.

Randomized Experiments

The defining characteristic of an experimental design is that units of study are randomly assigned either to a treatment (or intervention) group or to one or more nonparticipating control (or comparison) groups. Random assignment means that the assignment is made by chance, as in the flip of a coin, in order to control for any systematic difference between the groups that could account for a difference in their outcomes. A difference in these groups' subsequent outcomes is believed to represent the program's impact because, under random assignment, the factors that influence outcomes other than the program itself should be evenly distributed between the two groups; their effects tend to cancel one another out in a comparison of the two groups' outcomes. A true experiment is seldom, if ever, feasible for GAO because evaluators must have control over the process by which participants in a program are assigned to it, and this control generally rests with the agency. However, GAO does review experiments carried out by others.

Depending on how the program is administered, the unit of study might be such entities as a person, classroom, neighborhood, or industrial plant. More complex designs may involve two or more comparison groups that receive different combinations of services or experience the program at different levels of intensity. For example, patients might be randomly assigned to drug therapy, dietary, or exercise interventions to treat high blood pressure. For example,

- To evaluate the effect of the provision of housing assistance and employment support services on the capacity of low-income families to obtain or retain employment, the Department of Housing and Urban Development conducted a randomized experiment. In the sites chosen for the evaluation, eligible families on the waiting list for housing subsidies were randomly assigned either to an experimental group, who received a voucher and the employment support services bound to it, or to a control group, who did not receive a voucher or services. Both groups have been tracked for several years to determine the impact of the provision of rental assistance and accompanying services on families' employment, earnings, and geographic mobility (Abt Associates and QED Group 2004).

Limited Applicability of Randomized Experiments

Randomized experiments are best suited for assessing intervention or program effectiveness when it is possible, ethical, and practical to conduct and maintain random assignment to minimize the influence of external factors on program outcomes. Some kinds of interventions are not suitable for randomized assignment because the evaluator needs to have control over who will be exposed to it, and that may not be possible. Examples include interventions that use such techniques as public service announcements broadcast on the radio, television, or Internet. Random assignment is well suited for programs that are not universally available to the entire eligible population, so that some people will be denied access to services in any case, and a lottery is perceived as a fair way to form a comparison group.

Thus, no comparison group design is possible to assess full program impact where agencies are prohibited from withholding benefits from individuals entitled to them (such as veterans' benefits) or from selectively applying a law to some people but not others. Random assignment is often not accepted for testing interventions that prevent or mitigate harm because it is considered unethical to impose negative events or elevated risks of harm to test a remedy's effectiveness. Instead, the evaluator must wait for a hurricane or flood, for example, to learn if efforts to strengthen buildings prevented serious damage. (For further discussion, see GAO 2009, Rossi et al. 2004, or Shadish et al. 2002.)

Difficulties in Conducting Field Experiments

Field experiments are distinguished from laboratory experiments and experimental simulations in that field experiments take place in much less contrived, more naturalistic settings such as classrooms, hospitals, or workplaces. Conducting an inquiry in the field gives reality to the evaluation but often at the expense of some accuracy in the results. This is because experiments conducted in field settings allow limited control over both program implementation and external factors that may influence program results. In fact, enforcing strict adherence to program protocols in order to strengthen conclusions about program effects may actually limit the ability to generalize those conclusions to less perfect, but more typical program operations.

Ideally, randomized experiments in medicine are conducted as double-blind studies, in which neither the subjects nor the researchers know who is receiving the experimental treatment. However, double-blind studies in social science are uncommon, making it hard sometimes to distinguish the effects of a new program from the effects of introducing any novelty into the classroom or workplace. Moreover, program staff may jeopardize the random assignment process by exercising their own judgment in recruiting and enrolling participants. Because of the critical importance of the comparison groups' equivalence for drawing conclusions about program effects, it is important to check the effectiveness of random assignment by comparing the groups' equivalence on key characteristics before program exposure.

Comparison Group Quasi-experiments

Because of the difficulties in establishing a random process for assigning units of study to a program, as well as the opportunity provided when only a portion of the targeted population is exposed to the program, many impact evaluations employ a *quasi-experimental comparison group* design instead. This design also uses a treatment group and one or more comparison groups; however, unlike the groups in the true experiment, membership in these groups is not randomly assigned. Because the groups were not formed through a random process, they may differ with regard to other factors that affect their outcomes. Thus, it is usually not possible to infer that the "raw" difference in outcomes between the groups has been caused by the treatment. Instead, statistical adjustments such as analysis of covariance should be applied to the raw difference to compensate for any initial lack of equivalence between the groups.

Comparison groups may be formed from the pool of applicants who exceed the number of program slots in a given locale or from similar populations in other places, such as neighborhoods or cities, not served by the program. Drawing on the research literature to identify the key factors known to influence the desired outcomes will aid in forming treatment and comparison groups that are as similar as possible, thus strengthening the analyses' conclusions. When the treatment group is made up of volunteers, it is particularly important to address the potential for "selection bias"—that is, that volunteers or those chosen to participate will have greater motivation to succeed (for example, in attaining health, education, or employment outcomes) than those who were not accepted into the program. Statistical procedures, such as *propensity score analysis*, are used to statistically model the variables that influence participants' assignment to the program and are then applied to analysis of outcome data to reduce the influence of those variables on the program's estimated net impact. (For more information on propensity scores, see Rosenbaum 2002.) However, in the absence of random assignment, it is difficult to be sure that unmeasured factors did not influence differences in outcomes between the treatment and comparison groups.

A special type of comparison group design, *regression discontinuity analysis*, compares outcomes for a treatment and control group that are formed by having scores above or below a cut-point on a quantitative selection variable rather than through random assignment. When experimental groups are formed strictly on a cut-point and group outcomes are analyzed for individuals close to the cut-point, the groups can be left otherwise comparable except for the intervention. This technique is often used where the persons considered most "deserving" are assigned to the treatment, in order to address ethical concerns about denying services to persons in need—for example, when additional tutoring is provided only to children with the lowest reading scores. The technique requires a quantitative assignment variable that users believe is a credible selection criterion, careful control over assignment to ensure that a strict cut-point is achieved, large sample sizes, and sophisticated statistical analysis.

Difficulties in Conducting Comparison Group Experiments

Both experiments and quasi-experiments can be difficult to implement well in a variety of public settings. Confidence in conclusions about the program's impacts depends on ensuring that the treatment and comparison groups' experiences remain separate, intact, and distinct throughout the life of the study so that any differences in outcomes can be confidently attributed to the intervention. It is important to learn whether control group participants access comparable treatment in the community on their own. Their doing so could blur the distinction between the two groups' experiences. It is also preferred that treatment and control group members not communicate, because knowing that they are being treated differently might influence their perceptions of their experience and, thus, their behavior.

To resolve concerns about the ethics of withholding treatment widely considered beneficial, members of the comparison group are usually offered an alternative treatment or whatever constitutes common practice. Thus, experiments are usually conducted to test the efficacy of new programs or of new provisions or practices in an existing program. In this case, however, the evaluation will no longer be testing whether a new approach is effective *at all*; it will test whether it is more effective than standard practice.

In addition, comparison group designs may not be practical for some programs if the desired outcomes do not occur often enough to be observed within a reasonable sample size or study length. Studies of infrequent outcomes may require quite large samples to permit detection of a difference between the experimental and control groups. Because of the practical difficulties of maintaining intact experimental groups over time, experiments are also best suited for assessing outcomes within 1 to 2 years after the intervention, depending on the circumstances.

Statistical Analysis of Observational Data

Some federal programs and policies are not amenable to comparison group designs because they are implemented all at once, all across the country, with no one left untreated to serve in a comparison group. In such instances, quasi-experimental *single group designs* compare the outcomes for program participants before and after program exposure or the outcomes associated with natural variation in program activities, intensity or duration. In most instances, the simple version of a before-and-after design does not allow causal attribution of observed changes to exposure to the program because it is possible that other factors may have influenced those outcomes during the same time.

Before-and-after designs can be strengthened by adding more observations on outcomes. By taking many repeated observations of an outcome before and after an intervention or policy is introduced, an *interrupted time-series analysis* can be applied to the before-and-after design to help draw causal inferences. Long data series are used to smooth out the effects of random fluctuations over time. Statistical modeling of simultaneous changes in important external factors helps control for their influence on the outcome and, thus, helps isolate the impact of the intervention. This approach is used for full-coverage programs in which it may not be possible to find or form an untreated comparison group. The need for lengthy data series means the technique is used where the evaluator has access to long-term, detailed government statistical series or institutional records. For example,

- To assess the effectiveness of a product safety regulation in reducing injuries from a class of toys, the evaluator could analyze hospital records of injuries associated with these toys for a few years both before and after introduction of the regulation. To help rule out the influence of alternative plausible explanations, the evaluator might correlate these injury data with data on the size of the relevant age group and sales of these toys over the same time period.

An alternative observational approach is a cross-sectional study that measures the target population's exposure to the intervention (rather than controls its exposure) and compares the outcomes of individuals receiving different levels of the intervention. Statistical analysis is used to control for other plausible influences on the outcomes. Exposure to the intervention can be measured by whether a person was enrolled or how often a person participated in or was exposed to the program. This approach is used with full-coverage programs for which it is impossible to directly form treatment and control groups; nonuniform programs, in which different individuals are exposed differently; and interventions in which outcomes are observed too infrequently to make a prospective study practical. For example,

- An individual's annual risk of being in a car crash is so low that it would be impractical to randomly assign (and monitor) thousands of individuals to use (or not use) their seat belts in order to assess seat belts' effectiveness in preventing injuries during car crashes. Instead, the evaluator can analyze data on seat belt use and injuries in car crashes with other surveys on driver and passenger use of seat belts to estimate the effectiveness of seat belts in reducing injury.

Comprehensive Evaluations Explore Both Process and Results

Although this paper describes process and outcome evaluations as if they were mutually exclusive, in practice an evaluation may include multiple design components to address separate questions addressing both process and outcomes. In addition, comprehensive evaluations are often designed to collect both process and outcome information in order to understand the reasons for program performance and learn how to improve results. For example,

- Evaluators analyze program implementation data to ensure that key program activities are in place before collecting data on whether the desired benefits of the activities have been achieved.

- Evaluations of program effectiveness also measure key program components to help learn why a program is not working as well as was expected.

An evaluation may find that a program failed to achieve its intended outcomes for a variety of reasons, including: incomplete or poor quality implementation of the program; problems in obtaining valid and reliable data from the evaluation; environmental influences that blunt the program's effect; or the ineffectiveness of the program or intervention for the population and setting in which it was tested. Thus, examination of program implementation is very important to interpreting the results on outcomes. Moreover, because an impact evaluation may be conducted in a restricted range of settings in order to control for *other* influences on outcomes, its findings may not apply to other settings or subgroups of recipients. Thus, it is important to test the program or intervention's effects in several settings or under various circumstances before drawing firm conclusions about its effectiveness. A formal synthesis of the findings of multiple evaluations can provide important information about the limitations on—or factors influencing—program impacts, and be especially helpful in learning what works for whom and under what circumstances.

Designs for Different Types of Programs

As evaluation designs are tailored to the nature of the program and the questions asked, it becomes apparent that certain designs are necessarily excluded for certain types of programs. This is particularly true of impact evaluations because of the stringent conditions placed on the evidence needed to draw causal conclusions with confidence. Experimental research designs are best adapted to assess discrete interventions under carefully controlled conditions in the experimental physical and social sciences. The federal government has only relatively recently expanded its efforts to assess the effectiveness of all federal programs and policies, many of which fail to meet the requirements for successful use of experimental research designs.

To assist OMB officials in their efforts to assess agency evaluation efforts, an informal network of federal agency evaluators provided guidance on the relevance of various evaluation designs for different types of federal programs. Table 5 summarizes the features of the designs discussed in this chapter as well as the types of programs employing them.

Table 5: Designs for Assessing Effectiveness of Different Types of Programs

Typical design	Comparison controlling for alternative explanations	Best suited for
Process and outcome monitoring or evaluation	Performance and preexisting goals or standards, such as • R&D criteria of relevance, quality, and performance • productivity, cost effectiveness, and efficiency standards • customer expectations or industry benchmarks	Research, enforcement, information and statistical programs, business-like enterprises, and mature, ongoing programs where • coverage is national and complete • few, if any, alternatives explain observed outcomes
Quasi-experiments: single group	Outcomes for program participants before and after the intervention: • collects outcome data at multiple points in time • statistical adjustments or modeling control for alternative causal explanations	Regulatory and other programs where • clearly defined interventions have distinct starting times • coverage is national and complete • randomly assigning participants is NOT feasible, practical, or ethical
Quasi-experiments: comparison groups	Outcomes for program participants and a comparison group closely matched to them on key characteristics: • key characteristics are plausible alternative explanations for a difference in outcomes • measures outcomes before and after the intervention (pretest, posttest)	Service and other programs where • clearly defined interventions can be standardized and controlled • coverage is limited • randomly assigning participants is NOT feasible, practical, or ethical
Randomized experiments: control groups	Outcomes for a randomly assigned treatment group and a nonparticipating control group: • measures outcomes preferably before and after the intervention (pretest, posttest)	Service and other programs where • clearly defined interventions can be standardized and controlled • coverage is limited • randomly assigning participants is feasible and ethical

Source Adapted from Bernholz et al. 2006.

Some types of federal programs, such as those funding basic research projects or the development of statistical information, are not expected to have readily measurable effects on their environment. Therefore, research programs have been evaluated on the quality of their processes and products and relevance to their customers' needs, typically through expert peer review of portfolios of completed research projects. For example, the Department of Energy adopted criteria used or recommended by OMB and the National Academy of Sciences to assess research and development programs' relevance, quality, and performance (U.S. Department of Energy 2004.)

Regulatory and law enforcement programs can be evaluated according to the level of compliance with the pertinent rule or achievement of desired health or safety conditions, obtained through ongoing outcome monitoring. The effectiveness of a new law or regulation might be evaluated with a time-series design comparing health or safety conditions before and after its enactment, while controlling for other possible influences. Comparison group designs are not usually applied in this area because of unwillingness to selectively enforce the law.

Experimental and quasi-experimental impact studies are better suited for programs conducted on a small scale at selected locations, where program conditions can be carefully controlled, rather than at the national level. Such designs are particularly appropriate for demonstration programs testing new approaches or initiatives, and are not well suited for mature, universally available programs.

The next chapter outlines a number of approaches taken to evaluating federal programs that are not well suited to these most common designs, either because of the structure of the program or the context in which it operates.

For More Information

GAO documents	GAO. 1990. *Case Study Evaluations*, GAO/PEMD-10.1.9. Washington, D.C. November.
	GAO. 2003. *Federal Programs: Ethnographic Studies Can Inform Agencies' Actions*, GAO-03-455. Washington, D.C. March.
	GAO. 2009. *Program Evaluation: A Variety of Rigorous Methods Can Help Identify Effective Interventions*, GAO-10-30. Washington, D.C. Nov. 23.
	GAO. 2010. *Streamlining Government: Opportunities Exist to Strengthen OMB's Approach to Improving Efficiency*, GAO-10-394. Washington, D.C. May 7.
Other resources	Abt Associates and QED Group. 2004. *Evaluation of the Welfare to Work Voucher Program: Report to Congress*. U.S. Department of Housing and Urban Development, Office of Policy Development and Research. March.

Bernholz, Eric and others. 2006. *Evaluation Dialogue Between OMB Staff and Federal Evaluators: Digging a Bit Deeper into Evaluation Science.* Washington, D.C. July. http://www.fedeval.net/docs/omb2006briefing.pdf

Enders, Walter. 2009. *Applied Econometric Time Series*, 3rd ed. Hoboken, N.J.: Wiley.

Langbein, Laura and Claire L. Felbinger. 2006. *Public Program Evaluation: A Statistical Guide.* Armonk, N.Y.: M.E. Sharpe.

Lipsey, Mark W. "Theory as Method: Small Theories of Treatments." 1993. *New Directions for Program Evaluation* 57:5-38. Reprinted in 2007, *New Directions for Evaluation* 114:30-62.

OMB (U.S. Office of Management and Budget), Office of Information and Regulatory Affairs. 2006. *Standards and Guidelines for Statistical Surveys.* Washington, D.C. September. http://www.whitehouse.gov/omb/inforeg_statpolicy#pr

Rosenbaum, Paul R. 2002. *Observational Studies,* 2nd ed. New York: Springer.

Rossi, Peter H., Mark W. Lipsey, and Howard E. Freeman. 2004. *Evaluation: A Systematic Approach*, 7th ed. Thousand Oaks, Calif.: Sage.

Shadish, William R., Thomas D. Cook, and Donald T. Campbell. 2002. *Experimental and Quasi-Experimental Designs for Generalized Causal Inference.* Boston: Houghton Mifflin.

Stake, Robert E. 1995. *The Art of Case Study Research.* Thousand Oaks, Calif.: Sage.

U.S. Department of Energy. 2004. *Peer Review Guide: Based on a Survey of Best Practices for In-Progress Peer Review.* Prepared by the Office of Energy Efficiency and Renewable Energy Peer Review Task Force. Washington, D.C. August. http://www1.eere.energy.gov/ba/pba/pdfs/2004peerreviewguide.pdf.

Yin, Robert K. 2009. *Case Study Research: Design and Methods*, 4th ed. Thousand Oaks, Calif.: Sage.

Chapter 5: Approaches to Selected Methodological Challenges

Most of the impact designs discussed in chapter 4 were developed to test hypotheses about the causal effects of individual factors or discrete interventions on clearly defined outcomes. These designs may have limited relevance and credibility *on their own* for assessing the effects of federal programs where neither the intervention nor the desired outcome is clearly defined or measured. In addition, many, if not most, federal programs aim to improve some aspect of complex systems, such as the economy or the environment, over which they have limited control, or share responsibilities with other agencies for achieving their objectives. Thus, it can be difficult to confidently attribute a causal connection between the program and the observed outcomes. This chapter describes some of the evaluation strategies that federal agencies have used to develop performance information for these types of programs that can inform management, oversight, and policy.

Outcomes That Are Difficult to Measure

In many federal programs, it can be difficult to assess the program's effectiveness in achieving its ultimate objectives because it is difficult to obtain data on those goals. This can occur because there is no common measure of the desired outcome or because the desired benefits for the public are not frequently observed.

Challenge: Lack of Common Outcome Measures

A federal program might lack common national data on a desired outcome because the program is relatively new, new to measuring outcomes, or has limited control over how service providers collect and store information. Where state programs operate without much federal direction, outcome data are often not comparable across the states. Federal agencies have taken different approaches to obtaining common national outcome data, depending in part on whether such information is needed on a recurring basis (GAO 2003):

- collaborating with others on a common reporting format;

- recoding state data into a common format;

- conducting a special survey to obtain nation-wide data.

Collaborate with Others on a Common Reporting Format

Where federal programs operate through multiple local public or private agencies, careful collaboration may be required to ensure that the data they collect are sufficiently consistent to permit aggregation nationwide. To improve the quality and availability of substance abuse prevention and treatment, the Substance Abuse and Mental Health Services Administration (SAMHSA) awards block grants to states to help fund local drug and alcohol abuse programs. In order to measure progress towards national goals and the performance of programs administered by states' substance abuse and mental health agencies, SAMHSA funded pilot studies and collaborated with state agencies and service providers in developing national outcome measures for an ongoing performance monitoring system. The process of developing and agreeing upon data definitions has taken several years, but allows them to assess improvements in substance abuse treatment outcomes and monitor the performance of SAMHSA block grants. SAMHSA has also invested in states' data infrastructure improvement activities such as software, hardware, and training in how to use standardized data definitions (U.S. Department of Health and Human Services n.d.).

Recode State Data into a Common Format

Alternatively, if states already have their own distinct, mature data systems, it may not be practical to expect those systems to adopt new, common data definitions. Instead, to meet federal needs to assess national progress, a federal agency may choose to support a special data collection that abstracts data from state systems and recodes them into a common format, permitting cross-state and national analyses. For example, in order to analyze highway safety policies, the National Highway Traffic Safety Administration has invested in a nationwide system to extract data from state records to develop a well-accepted national database on fatal automobile crashes. A standard codebook provides detailed instructions on how to record data from state and local emergency room and police records into a common format that can support sophisticated analyses into the factors contributing to crashes and associated fatalities (GAO 2003). Although such a data collection and analysis system can be initially expensive to develop, it is likely to be less expensive to maintain such a system, and much more practical than attempting to gain agreements for data collection changes from hospitals and police departments across the country.

Conduct a Special Survey to Obtain Nation-Wide Data

Some federal agencies also, of course, conduct periodic sample surveys or one-time studies to collect new data that supplements data from existing performance reporting systems. For example, SAMHSA conducts a voluntary periodic survey of specialty mental health organizations that are not subject to the agency's routine grantee reporting requirements (U.S. Department of Health and Human Services n.d.). In addition, to obtain information on drug abusers who are not in treatment, they conduct an annual national household survey of drug use. Such surveys can provide valuable information about how well existing programs are serving the population's needs.

Challenge: Desired Outcomes Are Infrequently Observed

Some federal programs are created to respond to national concerns, such as increased cancer rates or environmental degradation, which operate in a lengthy time frame and are not expected to resolve quickly. Thus, changes in intended long-term outcomes are unlikely to be observed within an annual performance reporting cycle or even, perhaps, within a five-year evaluation study. Other programs aim to prevent or provide protection from events that are very infrequent and, most importantly, not predictable, such as storms or terrorist attacks, for which it is impractical to set annual or other relatively short-term goals. Evaluation approaches to these types of programs may rely heavily on well-articulated program logic models to depict the program's activities as multi-step strategies for achieving its goals. Depending on how infrequent or unexpected opportunities may be to observe the desired outcome, an evaluator might choose to:

- measure program effects on short-term or intermediate goals;

- assess the quality of an agency's prevention or risk management plan; or

- conduct a thorough after-action or critical-incident review of any incidents that do occur.

Measure Effects on Short-Term or Intermediate Goals

To demonstrate progress towards the program's ultimate goals, the evaluator can measure the program's effect on short-term and intermediate outcomes that are considered important interim steps towards achieving the program's long-term goals. This approach is particularly compelling when combined with findings from the research literature that confirms the relationship of short-term goals (such as increased vaccination rates) to the program's long-term goals (such as reduced incidence of communicable disease). (See GAO 2002 for examples.) Moreover, tracking performance trends and progress towards goals may provide timely feedback that can inform discussion of options for responding to emerging performance problems.

Assess the Quality of a Prevention or Risk Management Plan

Several federal programs are charged with managing risks that are infrequent but potentially quite dangerous, in a wide array of settings:

banking, intelligence, counter-terrorism, natural disasters, and community
health and safety. Generally, risk management involves:

- assessing potential threats, vulnerabilities of assets and networks,
  and the potential economic or health and safety consequences;

- assessing and implementing countermeasures to prevent incidents
  and reduce vulnerabilities to minimize negative consequences; and

- monitoring and evaluating their effectiveness (GAO 2005).

Depending on the nature of the threat, one federal program may focus
more on prevention (for example, of communicable disease) while
another focuses on response (for example, to hurricanes). Some threats
occur frequently enough that program effectiveness can be readily
measured as the reduction in threat incidents (such as car crashes) or
consequences (such as deaths and injuries). Where threat incidents do
not occur frequently enough to permit direct observation of the program's
success in mitigating their consequences, evaluators have a couple
choices.

The evaluator could assess the effectiveness of a risk-management
program through assessing (1) how well the program followed the
recommended "best practices" of design, including conducting a
thorough, realistic assessment of threats and vulnerabilities, and cost-
benefit analysis of alternative risk reduction strategies; and (2) how
thoroughly the agency implemented its chosen strategy, such as installing
physical protections or ensuring staff are properly trained.

Alternatively, an evaluator may choose to conduct simulations or
exercises to assess how well an agency's plans anticipate the nature of
its threats and vulnerabilities, as well as how well agency staff and
partners are prepared to carry out their responsibilities under their plans.
Exercises may be "table-top," where officials located in an office respond
to virtual reports of an incident, or "live," where volunteers act out the
roles of victims in public places to test the responses of emergency
services personnel. Exercises may be especially useful for obtaining a
realistic assessment of complex risk management programs that require
coordination among multiple agencies or public and private sector
organizations.

Conduct an After-Action or Critical-Incident Review

When a threat incident is observed, an evaluator can conduct an 'after-
action' or 'critical incident' review to assess the design and execution–or

effectiveness—of the prevention or risk mitigation program. The Army developed after-action reviews as a training methodology for soldiers to evaluate their performance against standards and develop insights into their strengths, weaknesses, and training needs (U.S. Department of the Army 1993). State and federal public safety agencies have adopted them to identify ways to improve emergency response. These reviews consist of a structured, open discussion of participants' observations of what occurred during an incident to develop 'lessons learned' about the effectiveness of plans and procedures and actionable recommendations. Reviews involve (1) detailed description of the nature and context of the incident and the actions taken and resources used step-by-step; followed by (2) a critique to assess whether plans and procedures were useful in addressing the incident and provide suggestions for improvement. These reviews may be formal—with an external facilitator or observer and a written report to management—or informal—conducted as an internal review to promote learning. Although identifying the factors contributing to success or failure in handling an incident could provide useful insight into the effectiveness of a risk mitigation program, the focus of these reviews is primarily on learning rather than judging program effectiveness.

Challenge: Benefits of Research Programs Are Difficult to Predict

With increased interest in assuring accountability for the value of government expenditures, have come increased efforts to demonstrate and quantify the value of public investments in scientific research. An evaluator might readily measure the effectiveness of an applied research program by whether it met its goal to improve the quality, precision, or efficiency of tools or processes. However, basic research programs do not usually have such immediate, concrete goals. Instead, goals for federal research programs can include advancing knowledge in a field, and building capacity for future advances through developing useful tools or supporting the scientific community. In addition, multiyear investments in basic research might be expected to lead to innovations in technology that will (eventually) yield social or financial value, such as energy savings or security. (For more information about methods for assessing these effects, see Ruegg and Jordan 2007.) Common agency approaches to evaluating research programs include:

- external expert review of a research portfolio;

- bibliometric analyses of research citations and patents.

External Expert Portfolio Review	To assess the quality of their research programs and obtain program planning advice, the National Science Foundation (NSF) adopted an external expert review process called a Committee of Visitors (COV) review. Periodically, panels of independent experts review the technical and managerial stewardship of a specific program (a portfolio of research projects), compare plans with progress made, and evaluate the outcomes to assess their contributions to NSF's mission and goals. COV reviews provide external expert judgments on 1) assessments of the quality and integrity of program operations and program-level technical and managerial matters pertaining to project decisions; and 2) comments on how the outputs and outcomes generated by awardees have contributed to NSF's mission and strategic outcome goals. Other federal science agencies have adopted similar expert panel reviews as independent evaluations of their basic research programs (U.S. Department of Energy 2004).
Bibliometric Analysis	Since publications and patents constitute major outputs of research programs and large databases capture these outputs, bibliometric analysis of research citations or patents is a popular way of assessing the productivity of research. In addition to simply tracking the quantity of publications, analysis of where, how often and by whom the papers are cited can provide information about the perceived relevance, impact and quality of the papers and can identify pathways of information flow.

Complex Federal Programs and Initiatives

Many federal programs are not discrete interventions aiming to achieve a specific outcome but, instead, efforts to improve complex systems over which they have limited control. Moreover, in the United States, federal and state governments often share responsibility for the direction of federal programs, so a federal program may not represent a uniform package of activities or services across the country.

Challenge: Benefits of Flexible Grant Programs Are Difficult to Summarize	Federal grant programs vary greatly as to whether they have performance objectives or a common set of activities across grantees such as state and local agencies or nonprofit service providers. Where a grant program represents a discrete program with a narrow set of activities and performance-related objectives, such as a food delivery program for seniors, it can often be evaluated with the methods described in chapter 4. However, a formula or 'block' grant, with loosely defined objectives that simply adds to a stream of funds supporting ongoing state or local programs, presents a significant challenge to efforts to portray the results

of the federal or 'national' program (GAO 1998a). Agencies have deployed a few distinct approaches, often in combination:

- describe national variation in local approaches;

- measure national improvement in common outputs or outcomes;

- conduct effectiveness evaluations in a sample of sites.

Describe National Variation in Local Approaches

An important first step in evaluating the performance of flexible grant programs is to describe the variation in approaches deployed locally, characteristics of the population served, and any information available on service outputs or outcomes. Depending on the nature of grantee reporting requirements, this information might be obtained from a review of federal program records or require a survey of grantees or local providers. Such descriptive information can be valuable in assessing how well the program met Congress' intent for the use and beneficiaries of those funds. In addition, where there is prior research evidence on the effectiveness of particular practices, this descriptive data can provide information, at least, on the extent to which grantees are deploying effective or 'research-based' practices.

Measure National Improvement in Common Outputs or Outcomes

Where the federal grant program has performance-related objectives but serves as a *funding stream* to support and improve the capacity of a state function or service delivery system, state (but not uniquely federal) program outcomes can be evaluated by measuring aggregate improvements in the quality of or access to services, outreach to the targeted population, or participant outcomes over time. Depending on the program, this information may be collected as part of state program administration, or require special data collection to obtain comparable data across states. For example, the Department of Education's National Assessment of Educational Progress tests a cross-sectional sample of children on a variety of key subjects, including reading and math, and regularly publishes state-by-state data on a set of common outcome measures. These national data also provide a comparative benchmark for the results of states' own assessments (Ginsburg and Rhett 2003). However, because cross-sectional surveys lack information linking specific use of federal funds to expected outcomes, they cannot assess the *effectiveness* of federal assistance in contributing to those service improvements; identifying those links is often very difficult in grant programs of this type.

Conduct Effectiveness Evaluations in a Sample of Sites

Some federal grant programs support distinct local projects to stimulate or test different approaches for achieving a performance objective. To assess such programs, the evaluator might study a sample of projects to assess their implementation and effectiveness in meeting their objectives. Individual impact evaluations might be arranged for as part of the original project grants, or conducted as part of a nationally-directed evaluation. Sites for evaluation might be selected purposively, to test the effectiveness of a variety of promising program approaches or represent the range in quality of services nationally (Herrell and Straw 2002).

For example, *cluster evaluations*, as used by the W. K. Kellogg Foundation, examine a loosely connected set of studies of community-based initiatives to identify common themes or components associated with positive impacts, and the reasons for such associations (W. K. Kellogg Foundation 2004). Cluster evaluations examine evidence of individual project effectiveness but do not aggregate that data across studies. *Multisite evaluations*, as frequently seen in federally-funded programs, may involve variation across sites in interventions and measures of project effectiveness, but typically use a set of common measures to estimate the effectiveness of the interventions and examine variation across sites in outcomes. (See discussion of comprehensive evaluations in chapter 4.) Both of these evaluation approaches are quite different from a *multicenter clinical trial* (or impact study) that conducts virtually the same intervention and evaluation in several sites to test the robustness of the approach's effects across sites and populations (Herrell and Straw 2002).

Case study evaluations, through providing more in-depth information about how a federal program operates in different circumstances, can serve as valuable supplements to broad surveys when specifically designed to do so. Case studies can be designed to follow-up on low or high performers, in order to explain–or generate hypotheses about—what is going on and why.

Challenge: Assess the Progress and Results of Comprehensive Reforms

In contrast to programs that support a particular set of activities aimed at achieving a specified objective, some comprehensive reform initiatives may call for collective, coordinated actions in communities in multiple areas such as altering public policy, improving service practice, or engaging the public to create system reform. This poses challenges to the evaluator in identifying the nature of the intervention (or program), the desired outcomes, as well as an estimate of what would have occurred in the absence of these reforms. Depending on the extent to which the dimensions of reform are well understood, the progress of reforms might be measured quantitatively in a survey or through a more exploratory form of case study.

Follow-up Survey Findings with Case Studies

For example, in the Department of Education's Comprehensive School Reform demonstration program, federal grantees were encouraged to strengthen several aspects of school operations—such as curriculum, instruction, teacher development, parental involvement—and to select and adopt models that had been found effective in other schools, in an effort to improve student achievement. The comprehensive evaluation of this program used three distinct methodological approaches to answer distinct questions about implementation and effects (U.S. Department of Education 2010)

1. Multivariate statistical analyses comparing grantees with matched comparison schools to determine whether receiving a grant was associated with student achievement level increases three to five years later;

2. Quantitative descriptive analyses of reform implementation from a survey of principals and teachers in a random sample of grantees and matched comparison schools to determine the comprehensiveness of reform implementation; and

3. Qualitative case study analyses to study reform component implementation and understand the process by which chronically low-performing schools turned themselves around and sustained student achievement gains.

Note that because a school reform effort by design applies to everyone in the school, the evaluators formed a comparison group by matching each grantee school with a school in another community with similar socio-economic characteristics. Moreover, this study's analyses of the schools' reforms were greatly assisted by being able to draw on the set of potential reforms listed in the legislation.

Conduct Exploratory Case Studies

A different approach is required for a much more open-ended program, such as the Department of Housing and Urban Development's Empowerment Zones and Enterprise Communities Program. This program provided grants and tax incentives to economically disadvantaged communities which were encouraged to develop their own individual economic development strategies around four key principles: economic opportunity, sustainable community development, community-based partnerships, and a strategic vision for change. Local evaluators assisted in collecting data in each of 18 case study sites to track how each community organized itself, set goals, and developed and implemented plans to achieve those goals–its *theory of change* (Fulbright-Anderson et al. 1998).

Case studies are recommended for assessing the effectiveness of comprehensive reforms that are so deeply integrated with the context (i.e., community) that no truly adequate comparison case can be found. In-depth interviews and observations are used to capture the changes in and relationships between processes, while outcomes may be measured quantitatively. The case study method is used to integrate this data into a coherent picture or story of what was achieved and how. In programs that are more direct about what local reform efforts are expected to achieve, the evaluator might provide more credible support for conclusions about program effects by: (1) making specific, refutable predictions of program effects, and (2) introducing controls for, or providing strong arguments against, other plausible explanations for observed outcomes. This theory of change approach cannot provide statistical estimates of effect sizes, but can provide detailed descriptions of the unfolding of the intervention and potential explanations for how and why the process worked to produce outcomes (Fulbright-Anderson et al. 1998, Yin and Davis 2007).

Challenge: Isolating Impact When Several Programs Are Aimed at the Same Outcome

Attributing observed changes in desired outcomes to the effect of a program requires ruling out other plausible explanations for those changes. Environmental factors such as historical trends in community attitudes towards smoking could explain changes in youths' smoking rates over time. Other programs funded with private, state, or other federal funds may also strive for similar goals to the program being evaluated. Although random assignment of individuals to treatment and comparison groups is intended to cancel out the influence of those factors, in practice, the presence of these other factors may still blur the effect of the program of interest or randomization may simply not be feasible. Collecting additional data and targeting comparisons to help rule out alternative explanations can help strengthen conclusions about an intervention's impact from both randomized and nonrandomized designs (GAO 2009, Mark and Reichardt 2004).

In general, to help isolate the impact of programs aimed at the same goal it can be useful to construct a logic model for each program—carefully specifying the programs' distinct target audiences and expected short-term outcomes—and to assess the extent to which the programs actually operate in the same localities and reach the same populations. Then the evaluator can devise a data collection approach or set of comparisons that could isolate the effects of the distinct programs, such as

- narrow the scope of the outcome measure;

- measure additional outcomes not expected to change;

- test hypothesized relationships between the programs.

Narrow the Scope of the Outcome Measure

Some programs have strategic goals that imply that they have a more extensive or broader range than they in fact do. By clarifying very specifically the program's target audience and expected behavior changes, the evaluator can select an outcome measure that is closely tailored to the most likely expected effects of the program and distinguish those effects from those of other related programs.

For example, to distinguish one antidrug media campaign from other antidrug messages in the environment, the campaign used a distinctive message to create a brand that would provide a recognizable element and improve recall. Then, the evaluation's survey asked questions about recognition of the brand, attitudes, and drug use so that analysis could correlate attitudes and behavior changes with exposure to this particular campaign (GAO 2002, Westat 2003).

In another example, the large number of workplaces in the country makes it impractical for the Occupational Safety and Health Administration to routinely perform health and safety inspections in all workplaces. Instead, program officials indicated that they target their activities to where they see the greatest problems—industries and occupations with the highest rates of fatality, injury, or illness. Thus, the agency set a series of performance goals that reflect differences in their expected influence, setting goals for reductions in three of the most prevalent injuries and illnesses and for injuries and illness in five "high-hazard" industries (GAO 1998b).

Measure Additional Outcomes Not Expected to Change

Another way to attempt to rule out plausible alternative explanations for observed results is to measure additional outcomes that a treatment or intervention is not expected to influence but arguably would be influenced under alternative explanations for the observed outcomes. If one can predict a relatively unique pattern of outcomes for the intervention, in contrast to the alternative, and if the study confirms that pattern, then the alternative explanation becomes less plausible. In a simple example, one can extend data collection either before or after the intervention to help rule out the influence of unrelated historical trends on the outcome of interest. If the outcome measure began to change before the intervention could have plausibly have affected it, then that change was probably influenced by some other factor.

Test Hypothesized Relationships between Programs

Some programs aimed at similar broad outcomes may be expected also to affect other programs. For example, the effectiveness of one program that aims to increase the number of medical personnel in locations considered medically underserved might be critical to ensuring that a second program to increase the number of patients with health insurance will result in their patients obtaining greater access to care. To assess the effectiveness of the health insurance program, the evaluator could survey potential recipients in a variety of locations where some are considered medically underserved and some are not. Interviews could follow-up on these hypotheses by probing reasons why potential recipients may have had difficulty obtaining needed health care.

For More Information

GAO documents

GAO. 1998a. *Grant Programs: Design Features Shape Flexibility, Accountability, and Performance Information,* GAO/GGD-98-137. Washington, D.C. June 22.

GAO. 1998b. *Managing for Results: Measuring Program Results That Are Under Limited Federal Control,* GAO/GGD-99-16. Washington, D.C. Dec. 11.

GAO. 2003. *Program Evaluation: An Evaluation Culture and Collaborative Partnerships Help Build Agency Capacity,* GAO-03-454. Washington, D.C. May 2.

GAO. 2009. *Program Evaluation: A Variety of Rigorous Methods Can Help Identify Effective Interventions,* GAO-10-30. Washington, D.C. Nov. 23.

GAO. 2002. *Program Evaluation: Strategies for Assessing How Information Dissemination Contributes to Agency Goals,* GAO-02-923. Washington, D.C. Sept. 30.

GAO. 2005. *Risk Management: Further Refinements Needed to Assess Risks and Prioritize Protective Measures at Ports and Other Critical Infrastructure.* GAO-06-91. Washington, D.C. Dec. 15.

Other resources

Domestic Working Group, Grant Accountability Project. 2005. *Guide to Opportunities for Improving Grant Accountability.* Washington, D.C.: U.S. Environmental Protection Agency, Office of Inspector General, October. www.epa.gov/oig/dwg/index.htm.

Fulbright-Anderson, Karen, Anne C. Kubisch, and James P. Connell, eds. 1998. *New Approaches to Evaluating Community Initiatives. vol. 2. Theory, Measurement, and Analysis.* Washington, D.C.: The Aspen Institute.

Ginsburg, Alan, and Nancy Rhett. 2003. "Building a Better Body of Evidence: New Opportunities to Strengthen Evaluation Utilization." *American Journal of Evaluation* 24: 489–98.

Herrell, James M., and Roger B. Straw, eds. 2002. Conducting Multiple Site Evaluations in Real-World Settings. *New Directions for Evaluation* 94. San Francisco: Jossey-Bass, Summer.

Mark, Melvin M. and Charles S. Reichardt. 2004. "Quasi-Experimental and Correlational Designs: Methods for the Real World When Random Assignment Isn't Feasible." In Carol Sansone, Carolyn C. Morf, and A. T. Panter, eds. *The Sage Handbook of Methods in Social Psychology.* Thousand Oaks, Calif.: Sage.

Ruegg, Rosalie, and Gretchen Jordan. 2007. *Overview of Evaluation Methods for R&D Programs: A Directory of Evaluation Methods Relevant to Technology Development Programs.* Prepared under contract DE-AC0494AL8500. Washington, D.C.: U.S. Department of Energy, Office of Energy Efficiency and Renewable Energy. March.

U.S. Department of Education, Office of Planning, Evaluation and Policy Development, Policy and Program Studies Service. 2010. *Evaluation of the Comprehensive School Reform Program Implementation and Outcomes: Fifth Year Report.* Washington, D.C.

U.S. Department of Energy. 2004. *Peer Review Guide: Based on a Survey of Best Practices for In-Progress Peer Review.* Prepared by the Office of Energy Efficiency and Renewable Energy Peer Review Task

Force. Washington, D.C.: August.
http://www1.eere.energy.gov/ba/pba/pdfs/2004peerreviewguide.pdf.

U.S. Department of Health and Human Services, Substance Abuse and
Mental Health Services Administration. n.d. *SAMHSA Data Strategy: FY
2007- FY2011.* Washington, D.C.

U.S. Department of Homeland Security, Federal Emergency Management
Agency, U.S. Fire Administration. 2008. *Special Report: The After-Action
Critique: Training Through Lessons Learned.* Technical Report Series.
USFA-TR-159. Emmitsburg, Md.: April.

U.S. Department of the Army, Headquarters. 1993. *A Leader's Guide to
After-Action Reviews,* Training Circular 25-20. Washington, D.C.:
September 30. http://www.au.af.mil/au/awc/awcgate

W. K. Kellogg Foundation. 2004. *W. K. Kellogg Foundation Evaluation
Handbook.* Battle Creek, Mich.: Jan. 1, 1998, updated.
http://www.wkkf.org/knowledge-center/resources/2010/W-K-Kellogg-
Foundation-Evaluation-Handbook.aspx

Westat. 2003. *Evaluation of the National Youth Anti-Drug Media
Campaign: 2003 Report of Findings.* Prepared under contract N01DA-8-
5063. Rockville, Md.: National Institutes of Health, National Institute on
Drug Abuse, Dec. 22.

Yin, Robert K. and Darnella Davis 2007. "Adding New Dimensions to
Case Study Evaluations: The Case of Evaluating Comprehensive
Reforms." *New Directions for Evaluation* 113:75-93.

Appendix I: Evaluation Standards

Different auditing and evaluation organizations have developed guidelines or standards to help ensure the quality, credibility, and usefulness of evaluations. Some standards pertain specifically to the evaluator's organization (for example, auditor independence), the planning process (for example, stakeholder consultations), or reporting (for example, documenting assumptions and procedures). While the underlying principles substantially overlap, the evaluator will need to determine the relevance of each guideline to the evaluator's organizational affiliation and the specific evaluation's scope and purpose.

"Yellow Book" of Government Auditing Standards

GAO publishes generally accepted government auditing standards (GAGAS) for the use of individuals in government audit organizations conducting a broad array of work, including financial and performance audits. The standards are broad statements of auditors' (or evaluators') responsibilities in an overall framework for ensuring that they have the competence, integrity, objectivity, and independence needed to plan, conduct, and report on their work. The standards use "performance audit" to refer to "an independent assessment of the performance and management of government programs against objective criteria or an assessment of best practices and other information"; thus, it is intended to include program process and outcome evaluations.

The general standards applying to all financial and performance audits include the independence of the audit organization and its individual auditors; the exercise of professional judgment; competence of staff; and the presence of quality control systems and external peer reviews. The field work standards for performance audits relate to planning the audit; supervising staff; obtaining sufficient, competent, and relevant evidence; and preparing audit documentation.

GAO. 2011. *Government Auditing Standards: 2011 Internet Version*. Washington, D.C.: August. http://www.gao.gov/govaud/iv2011gagas.pdf

GAO's Evaluation Synthesis

GAO's transfer paper *The Evaluation Synthesis* lists illustrative questions for assessing the soundness of each study's basic research design, conduct, analysis, and reporting—regardless of the design employed. The questions address the clarity and appropriateness of study design, measures, and analyses and the quality of the study's execution and reporting.

GAO.1992. *The Evaluation Synthesis,* revised, GAO/PEMD-10.1.2. Washington, D.C.: March.

American Evaluation Association Guiding Principles for Evaluators

The American Evaluation Association (AEA) is a professional association with U.S. headquarters for evaluators of programs, products, personnel, and policies. AEA developed guiding principles for the work of professionals in everyday practice and to inform evaluation clients and the general public of expectations for ethical behavior. The principles are broad statements of evaluators' responsibilities in five areas: *systematic inquiry; competence; honesty and integrity; respect for people*; and *responsibilities for general and public welfare.*

AEA. 2004. *Guiding Principles for Evaluators.* July. http://www.eval.org/Publications/GuidingPrinciples.asp.

Program Evaluation Standards, Joint Committee on Standards for Educational Evaluation

A consortium of professional organizations (including the American Evaluation Association), the Joint Committee on Standards for Educational Evaluation, developed a set of standards for evaluations of educational programs, which have been approved as an American National Standard. The standards are organized into five major areas of concern: to ensure program stakeholders find evaluations valuable *(utility)*; to increase evaluation effectiveness and efficiency *(feasibility);* to support what is proper, fair, legal, right, and just in evaluations *(propriety)*; to increase the dependability and truthfulness of evaluation representations and findings *(accuracy)*; and to encourage accurate documentation and a focus on improvement and accountability of evaluation processes and products *(evaluation accountability)*.

Yarbrough, D. B., L. M. Shulha, R. K. Hopson, and F. A. Caruthers. 2011. *The Program Evaluation Standards: A Guide for Evaluators and Evaluation Users,* 3rd ed. Thousand Oaks, Calif.: Sage.

Appendix II: GAO Contact and Staff Acknowledgments

GAO Contact	Nancy Kingsbury (202) 512-2700 or kingsburyn@gao.gov
Staff Acknowledgments	In addition to the person named above, Stephanie Shipman, Assistant Director, made significant contributions to this report. Additional contributors include Thomas Clarke, Timothy Guinane, Penny Pickett, and Elaine Vaurio.

Other Papers in This Series

Assessing the Reliability of Computer-Processed Data, external version 1, GAO-09-680G. Washington, D.C.: July 2009.

Case Study Evaluations, GAO/PEMD-10.1.9, November 1990.

How to Get Action on Audit Recommendations, OP-9.2.1, July 1991.

Performance Measurement and Evaluation: Definitions and Relationships, GAO-11-646SP, May 2011.

Prospective Evaluation Methods: The Prospective Evaluation Synthesis, GAO/PEMD-10.1.10, November 1990.

Quantitative Data Analysis: An Introduction, GAO/PEMD-10.1.11, May 1992.

Record Linkage and Privacy: Issues in Creating New Federal Research and Statistical Information, GAO-01-126SP, April 2001.

The Evaluation Synthesis, revised, GAO/PEMD-10.1.2, March 1992.

The Results Act: An Evaluator's Guide to Assessing Agency Annual Performance Plans, version 1, GAO/GGD-10.1.20, April 1998.

Using Statistical Sampling, revised, GAO/PEMD-10.1.6, May 1992.

Using Structured Interviewing Techniques, GAO/PEMD-10.1.5, June 1991.

GAO's Mission	The Government Accountability Office, the audit, evaluation, and investigative arm of Congress, exists to support Congress in meeting its constitutional responsibilities and to help improve the performance and accountability of the federal government for the American people. GAO examines the use of public funds; evaluates federal programs and policies; and provides analyses, recommendations, and other assistance to help Congress make informed oversight, policy, and funding decisions. GAO's commitment to good government is reflected in its core values of accountability, integrity, and reliability.
Obtaining Copies of GAO Reports and Testimony	The fastest and easiest way to obtain copies of GAO documents at no cost is through GAO's website (www.gao.gov). Each weekday afternoon, GAO posts on its website newly released reports, testimony, and correspondence. To have GAO e-mail you a list of newly posted products, go to www.gao.gov and select "E-mail Updates."
Order by Phone	The price of each GAO publication reflects GAO's actual cost of production and distribution and depends on the number of pages in the publication and whether the publication is printed in color or black and white. Pricing and ordering information is posted on GAO's website, http://www.gao.gov/ordering.htm. Place orders by calling (202) 512-6000, toll free (866) 801-7077, or TDD (202) 512-2537. Orders may be paid for using American Express, Discover Card, MasterCard, Visa, check, or money order. Call for additional information.
Connect with GAO	Connect with GAO on Facebook, Flickr, Twitter, and YouTube. Subscribe to our RSS Feeds or E-mail Updates. Listen to our Podcasts. Visit GAO on the web at www.gao.gov.
To Report Fraud, Waste, and Abuse in Federal Programs	Contact: Website: www.gao.gov/fraudnet/fraudnet.htm E-mail: fraudnet@gao.gov Automated answering system: (800) 424-5454 or (202) 512-7470
Congressional Relations	Katherine Siggerud, Managing Director, siggerudk@gao.gov, (202) 512-4400, U.S. Government Accountability Office, 441 G Street NW, Room 7125, Washington, DC 20548
Public Affairs	Chuck Young, Managing Director, youngc1@gao.gov, (202) 512-4800 U.S. Government Accountability Office, 441 G Street NW, Room 7149 Washington, DC 20548

Please Print on Recycled Paper.